Yoga Sutras of Patanjali

The Ultimate Guide to Learn Yoga Philosophy, Expand Your Mind and Increase Your Emotional Intelligence - The Unspoken Truths About Yoga Meditation

MARILYN GILLIAN

Copyright © 2020 MARILYN GILLIAN

All rights reserved.

The content contained within this book may not be reproduced, duplicated or transmitted without direct written permission from the author or the publisher.

Under no circumstances will any blame or legal responsibility be held against the publisher, or author, for any damages, reparation, or monetary loss due to the information contained within this book, either directly or indirectly.

Legal Notice:
This book is copyright protected. It is only for personal use. You cannot amend, distribute, sell, use, quote or paraphrase any part, or the content within this book, without the consent of the author or publisher.

Disclaimer Notice:
Please note the information contained within this document is for educational and entertainment purposes only. All effort has been executed to present accurate, up to date, reliable, complete information. No warranties of any kind are declared or implied. Readers acknowledge that the author is not engaged in the rendering of legal, financial, medical or professional advice. The content within this book has been derived from various sources. Please consult a licensed professional before attempting any techniques outlined in this book.

By reading this document, the reader agrees that under no circumstances is the author responsible for any losses, direct or indirect, that are incurred as a result of the use of the information contained within this document, including, but not limited to, errors, omissions, or inaccuracies.

Table of Contents

Chapter 1: Modern Challenges, Ancient Strategies in Reading the YOGA Sutra in the Twenty-First Century 1

    What can sutra YOGA maybe go about, if not YOGA? 2

Chapter 2: Patanjali, the YOGA Sutra and Indian Philosophy 14

Chapter 3: How YOGA Sutra was Discovered in the West 31

Chapter 4: Your Perception determines Your Belief System: The Cosmic Drama 46

    Purusha: Pure Unbounded Consciousness 49

    Prakriti: Undifferentiated Matter 50

    Avidya: Spiritual Ignorance 50

    Sri Patanjali 52

Chapter 5: Now, let us have an exposition of YOGA 55

    YOGA 56

    Chitta 58

    Buddhi: two implications 59

    Vritti 60

        Nirodha 69

        With nirodha 70

        Without nirodha 70

Chapter 6: The Seer and Other Related Concepts 76

    By Category 78

    By Effect 78

Direct Perception 81

  Inference 83

  Authoritative Testimony.. 86

  Comparison between Misperception and Conceptualization
 93

  Memory is the memory of experienced items 95

  Experience It 99

  Long Time 102

  Without Break 102

  With Enthusiasm... 103

Chapter 7: Nonattachment.. 106

Chapter 8: Samadhis of the YOGA Sutras 111

  Examination..115

  Insight...116

  Joy...117

  Pure I-am-ness 117

  Faith 120

  Strength 123

  Mindfulness 124

Chapter 9: How to Attain Samadhi with Devotion and Total Dedication to God (Ishwara).. 128

  Unconditioned by time, Ishwara is the instructor of even the most ancient educators... 133

  The expression of Ishwara is the mystic sound OM. 137

    Mantras 138

    OM... 139

    Universality of OM..141

Chapter 10: Distractions and Obstacles 144
  Disease... 144
  Weakness 145
  Uncertainty 145
  Carelessness... 146
  Laziness 147
  Sensuality 147
  Bogus Perception 147
  Failing to Attain Firm Ground 148
  Slipping from the Ground Reached................................ 148
Chapter 11: Locks and Keys of Life 158
  Lock 1: Happiness; The Key: Friendliness...................... 158
  Lock 2: Unhappiness; The Key: Compassion 159
  Lock 3: Virtuous; The Key: Delight 160
  Lock 4: Nonvirtuous; Key: Equanimity.......................... 161
Chapter 12: The benefits of YOGA sutras........................165
  A Good Heart Functioning..170
  Lowering the blood sugar level by YOGA 171
  YOGA as a stress buster 172
  YOGA also makes you focus 173
  YOGA is a memory booster. 173
  Spiritual Benefits of YOGA..174
  YOGA teaches one how the Kundalini is awake 174
  How YOGA benefits when it comes to preventing a disease
 175
  YOGA reduces the risk of Alzheimer's............................175

Chapter 12: The best practices in YOGA Sutras 177
Chapter 13: Best times of the day to do YOGA 184
Conclusion 189
    Brahmacharya - Pure way 190
    Aparigrapha – Nonassociation with Possessions 190
    Niyama which consist of five principles; 191
    Santosh- contentment 191

Chapter 1: Modern Challenges, Ancient Strategies in Reading the YOGA Sutra in the Twenty-First Century

In the United States, an expected 17 million individuals routinely go to YOGA classes, there is a developing pattern among YOGA teachers, individuals who learn in a huge number of YOGA and study focuses that spread the nation over. Educator preparing regularly incorporates "Mando Tory" and directions on YOGA Sutra in Patanelli. This is in any event fascinating, given the way that tomorrow's YOGA is pertinent to YOGA, as he adapted today, as an understanding, that everything is in the ignition machine, driving the vehicle.

The inquiry is: Why? Why String (that is what tomorrow's statement implies in Sanskrit, the language of YOGA tomorrow) from 195 Abbey, made in the main hundreds of years of Com-Mon ERA to be perused by the YOGA teacher in the 21st century? What an old reaction to exit by genuine information may have something to do with present day postural YOGA, or the treatment and extending and breathing we call YOGA tomorrow today? The undeniable answer, many states, is for the sake of Patangene's work.

What can sutra YOGA maybe go about, if not YOGA?

YOGA has been a global word for more than 200 years. The French teacher Gaston-Laurent Coeurdoux is synonymous with "Yoham" from India" with "Betion" in the seventeenth century. In his 1785 interpretation of Bhagavad Gita, the British Orientalist Charles Wilkins didn't give interpretations to the words "Ukrainian" or "Yogee", for reasons that will be seen later right now. "The YOGA" had the German word for over a century, "Il YOGA" the Italian word, etc.

Obviously, YOGA was initially a Sanskrit word, so you'd figure it is sufficient to open a Sanskrit lexicon to comprehend what YOGA is. Since its distribution in 1899, Sir Monier-Williams' Sanskrit English Dictionary has been a standard reference for first-year understudies and experienced researchers to interpret Sanskrit words. Also, what do we find when we take a gander at the "YOGA" entrance right now? Weighs around 2,500 words, it is perhaps the longest passage in the whole lexicon, takes four sections print. 72 of these words depict the utilization of the expression "YOGA" in Sutra YOGA. At last, coming up next are included:

Application or centralization of the psyche, theoretical contemplation and mental withdrawal practice bound as a framework (as scholarly by Patanjali and theory of YOGA; This is the second of two Samkhya frameworks, its fundamental reason for existing is to show the methods by which the human brain can accomplish full association with Isvara or with the most noteworthy soul; practically speaking, self-fixation is presently connected with Buddhism).

Right now, is in any event one imperfection that I will return to later, however first increasingly about the general shared characteristic of YOGA. (Right now, will acquire "YOGA" on the off chance that I consider YOGA a philosophical framework, while I will utilize lowercase letters for every single other utilization of the term.) In agreement with the authoritative standards of lexicons of this sort, Monier-Williams starts his YOGA contribution with his most seasoned and most regularly utilized implications before changing to later and progressively constrained use. In a specific order, his meaning of YOGA showed up soon after a not insignificant rundown of increasingly normal implications, which, repeated here, were perused as a rundown that Jorge Luis Borges could have longed for from the "Babel Library" that he owned:

YOGA: act of yoking or joining something together with another. E.g putting in (from horses); team, vehicle, transport; employing, using, applications, performance; equipping or indicting (armies); Repair (from arrows to bowstring); placing (of armor); medicine, medicine; means, accelerated, device, in, in, in, method; supernatural agents, poor, incantation, magic to art; trick, stray, fraud; endeavor, work; Acquisition, profit, wealth, assets; opportunity, opportunity; any crossroads, Union, connection, contact with; the mixing of various materials, brass; paruzo, possession; connection, connection (resulting, on the basis, by the basis, accordingly, accordingly, through); We're putting together, we're working on it. fit into common, fitness, decency, suitability (appropriate, proper, fair, in the right way); effort, effort, Zeal, Diligence, industry, care, care (hard work).

Before we desert Sir Monier, it ought to be noticed that stances, extending, and breathing are discovered nowhere here (in spite of the fact that they are implied in his meaning of Hatha YOGA, in a different passage). With this, let us come back to our unique inquiry of why it is—the point at which the "YOGA Sutra definition" of YOGA is anything but an especially early or significant one, and when the substance of the YOGA Sutra are almost without conversation of stances, extending, and breathing while many other Sanskrit works with "YOGA" in their titles are dedicated to those very practices—that guidance in the YOGA Sutra ought to be necessary for current YOGA educators?

We may begin by putting this front line allotment of Patanjali's work in its chronicled setting. Since the hour of its game plan, the YOGA Sutra has been deciphered by three noteworthy social events: the YOGA Sutra's old style Indian examiners; momentum fundamental analysts; and people from the forefront YOGA subculture, including experts and their supporters. A fourth assembling, clear by its nonattendance, should in like manner be referenced here. For reasons that we will see, the people commonly known as "yogis" have had in every practical sense no interest or stake in the YOGA Sutra or YOGA theory. A clear separation point partitions the gatherings just referenced. From one perspective, current basic researchers, who read the YOGA Sutra as a philosophical work, concern themselves almost solely with the old style commentators and their readings of the work's axioms. On the other, there are the disciples of the advanced YOGA subculture, who by and large read the YOGA Sutra as a manual for their postural practice, yet whose under- remaining of the work is refracted not through the traditional analyses themselves, yet rather through Hindu sacred writing. Here, I am talking basically of the incomparable Mahabharata epic and the Puranas ("Antiquarian Books"), gigantic medieval reference books of Hindu idea and practice. Accordingly, these equal universes of translation combine on however a solitary point; that point being what Patanjali named the "eight--part practice" (ashtanga--YOGA), his progression -by--step manual for reflection. Notwithstanding, for reasons unknown, the two voting demographics regardless have separated over even this little point, as in the old style pundits and basic researchers have made a decision about this to be the least huge bit of the YOGA Sutra, while the cutting edge YOGA subculture has concentrated only on the eight--part practice. As we will find in the following section, most scriptural records of the eight--part practice really subverted Patanjali's lessons, adding to the virtual eradication of YOGA as a reasonable philosophical framework by the sixteenth century. At that point, through a progression of im- plausible cooperative energies, YOGA rose from its remains in the late nineteenth century to turn into a faction object for a great part of the cutting edge YOGA subculture.

In contrast to the Mahabharata and the Puranas, which are unknown arrangements of old Hindu hallowed legend, the old style editorials on the YOGA Sutra are "marked" works by authentic figures. Most researchers accept that the soonest among these, a certain Vyasa, composed his critique inside many years of the appearance of the YOGA Sutra. Be that as it may, others contend he lived upwards of 600 years after Patanjali: we will return to the topic of Vyasa's dates in the last part of this book. The YOGA Sutra's other significant discourses date from between the ninth and sixteenth hundreds of years; be that as it may, no critique was written with regards to the YOGA framework after the twelfth century, which might be taken as a tipping point following which the school started to fall into decay (aside from a restricted YOGA "recovery" in south India, between the sixteenth and eighteenth hundreds of years).

We know from their scriptures that the commentators of old were splendid, gigantically developed people had of an intensive handle of India's customary treasury of information. About all were rationalists and schoolmen who, writing in the Sanskrit medium, looked to unload the importance of Patanjali's adages and safeguard their readings of its message against the cases of opponent scholars and schools, of which there were many. Notwithstanding teaching their understudies in illustrious courts, brahmanic universities, isolations, sanctuaries, and cloisters, they would have likewise partaken in banters on the extraordinary inquiries of the time, conveying forward a training that dated back to the Vedas (ca. 1500–1000 BCE), the most antiquated wellsprings of Hindu disclosure. This we know in light of the fact that a large number of their critiques hold a discussion design, presenting their foes' points of view so as to accordingly counter them with their own contentions. Discussions could be energetic undertakings in these unique situations, "reasoning hammers" whose victors were regularly compensated with riches, position, and brilliance.

Each extraordinary content in India has been the object of one, if not a few such discourses. As a rule, these are profoundly specialized treatises that break down the terms and ideas introduced in unique sacred texts, for example, (for Hindus) the Vedas, Upanishads, Bhagavad Gita, and major philosophical works. Here, the sign of a decent observer is his objectivity, his capacity to impartially come to his meaningful conclusions about a content in the light not just of the language of the content itself yet additionally of different analyses that have gone before his own. All things considered, critiques are, notwithstanding being interpretations of contemporary discussions, discussions with their past, where prior purposes of conversation are broken down through cautious point of reference-based contention. While through and through development is an irregularity in old style editorial, changing philosophical and true settings make for steady moves in the apparent implications of the words and ideas being deciphered, with the end goal that after some time—and here I am talking about hundreds, if not a great many years—the commentarial "huge picture" of a given work is bit by bit adjusted, in some cases to the point of being unrecognizable.

One finds a comparative circumstance in Western legitimate conventions, in what is known as legal audit in the United States. Legal audit expect that the chief wellsprings of the American lawful framework—English customary law, the Magna Carta, and in particular, the Constitution—structure a living convention where legal points of reference are reworked in the light of changing genuine -world settings. Central ideas, for example, "free discourse," "citizenship," and the "option to carry weapons," are continually being tried and retested through legal survey, changing even as they continue as before. Likewise, with Patanjali's work, it is highly unlikely to return to the "first goal" of the composers of the Constitution, which is immaterial regardless, in light of the fact that their reality was not equivalent to our own today. In numerous regards, basic YOGA researchers are the advanced -day homologues of the traditional pundits whose works they study.

In the course of recent years specifically, basic grant on YOGA has become a development industry in the American and European institutes. So as to be paid attention to in the foundation, the basic researcher must work with essential source material, which on account of the YOGA Sutra has implied the sutras themselves as well as other Sanskrit language takes a shot at YOGA and united philosophical frameworks, and, most importantly, the work's old style editorials. Here, basic YOGA grant essentially comprises of the meticulous assignment of parsing the manners in which that the words and ideas of the YOGA Sutra have been deciphered after some time, so as to coax out examples of impact and change. At that point follows the procedure of the basic survey of insightful thoughts in scholarly colloquia and through diary articles, book audits, etc.

A noteworthy number of principally North American YOGA researchers have likewise been professionals of YOGA, and numerous if not the greater part of these were first brought into the investigation of the YOGA Sutra through their own training. Regularly, their readings of the YOGA Sutra will fall some place in the middle of those of nonpracticing basic researchers and individuals from the more extensive YOGA subculture. One relies on which these researcher experts will in general can't help contradicting their nonpracticing associates concerns the significance of Vyasa to a right comprehension of the YOGA Sutra. Vyasa was the soonest as well as by a wide margin the most generally cited of all the old style YOGA Sutra pundits.

To start, Patanjali utilizes a few specialized Sanskrit terms in manners that are exceptional to the YOGA Sutra. Furthermore, the language of the sutras is frequently nearer to what has been named "Buddhist Hybrid Sanskrit"— that is, the Sanskrit of the early Mahayana Buddhist sacred texts of the principal hundreds of years of the Common Era—than to the old style Sanskrit of almost every Hindu sacred writing and discourse.

Further confusing issues is the way that there are just four action words in the whole work! This is the place Vyasa's critique ends up being a valuable asset. Complete sentences require action words, and Vyasa accommodatingly supplies the missing action words and significantly more.

This isn't completely extraordinary. In India, the aphoristic style of sutra--type lessons have generally been utilized as mental helpers for discussing and reviewing to memory the focal fundamentals of a given philosophical or strict framework. In any case, without the supplement of a living master's instructing, or, bombing that, a composed critique, the sayings regularly stay invulnerable. No doubt they were confounding to the YOGA Sutra's old style observers also. Thusly, about each editorial on the work is really a subcommentary, that is, a treatise that remarks on Vyasa's "approved" understanding as opposed to on Patanjali's work itself. Vyasa's critique on the YOGA Sutra was not, be that as it may, totally impartial or straightforward, since he, truth be told, put together it with respect to the power of an alternate, however related, philosophical framework known as Samkhya. This has incalculably affected how individuals have perused the YOGA Sutra, since they have really been perusing it through the viewpoint of Vyasa's Samkhya--inflected analysis. So it is that quite a bit of what perusers take to be the YOGA Sutra's essential jargon— the words Purusha (actually "the Man" or "Individual," yet frequently deciphered as "Soul"), Prakriti ("Nature, Matter, Materiality," a ladylike word in Sanskrit), buddhi ("insight"), and ahamkara ("self image")— are for all intents and purposes missing from Patanjali's work however ubiquitous in Vyasa and well over a thousand years of succeeding editorial and scholarship. Edwin Bryant has abridged the circumstance in the accompanying terms:

So when we discuss the way of thinking of Patanjali,

what we truly mean (or should mean) is the comprehension of Patanjali as per Vyasa: It is Vyasa who figured out what Patanjali's recondite sutras implied, and every consequent observer explained on Vyasa... It can't be exaggerated that YOGA reasoning is Patanjali's way of thinking as comprehended and verbalized by Vyasa. To give yet a solitary case of the upsetting issues the YOGA Sutra presents for any individual who might attempt to enter its significance, we may take a gander at the manners by which individuals have interpreted its all--important second sutra into English. This current, Patanjali's smaller meaning of YOGA, is made out of four words: YOGA--citta--vritti-- nirodha. Of course, there are no action words right now, we are within the sight of a juxtaposition: YOGA = citta + vritti + nirodha. While "citta" has a wide scope of implications in early Sanskrit, the most satisfactory non- specialized interpretation of the term is "thought." As for "vritti," it signifies "turning," and is identified with the - -vert in the English words contemplative person ("turned internal") and social butterfly ("turned outward") just as transform, subvert, distort, return, etc. Nirodha is a term meaning "stoppage" or "limitation" in Sanskrit. A basic interpretation of YOGA--citta--vritti--nirodha should then peruse something like "YOGA is the stoppage of the turn-ings of thought." But straightforward isn't the principal word that rings a bell when taking a gander at the manners in which individuals have understood this or different sutras of Patanjali's work.

Given its strong economic and basic history and the

high regard in which it and its creator are held by researchers, passionate Hindus, and the advanced-day YOGA subculture in the two India and the West, one may accept that the YOGA Sutra has been, similar to the Bible for Christians and Jews, a lasting Indian "great." As will be appeared in the parts that follow, this has not been the situation. For a few hundred years preceding its "disclosure" by a British Orientalist in the mid-1800s, the YOGA Sutra had been a lost convention. Subsequently, recorders had quit duplicating YOGA Sutra original copies (in light of the fact that nobody minded to understand them) and guidance in YOGA reasoning had been dropped from the customary Hindu educational program (on the grounds that nobody minded to recount or retain the sutras). In the wake of this long rest, the "recuperation" that followed the content's rediscovery was a tormented procedure, producing a lot of sound and fierceness, regularly meaning nothing, as its numerous cutting-edge translators anticipated their dreams, assumptions, expectations, dreams, and individual motivation onto Patanjali's work in uncommon manners. Therefore, the YOGA Sutra has been some-thing of a battered vagrant for the majority of the most recent two centuries, frequently mishandled by well--meaning or not--so--well--meaning specialists and trifler, spiritualists and realists, reformers and reactionaries who have taken advantage of it as a wellspring of political, scholarly, or emblematic capital.

A significant part of the equalization of this book will be committed to following the cracked history of these cutting edge allotments and contestations, which have conveyed the YOGA Sutra's heritage over the seas and over the cold pinnacles of the Himalayan Shangrila, crisscrossing between Kolkata, London, Berlin, Varanasi, Chicago, New York, Chennai, Mysore, Los Angeles, and many, many, puts in the middle. Most inquisitively—and this is the thing that sets the YOGA Sutra and its philosophical framework separated from each other Indian school—is this isn't the first occasion when that Patanjali's work has been conveyed a long way past the outskirts of the Indian subcontinent. This had just happened in the tenth and eleventh hundreds of years, when broad YOGA Sutra analyses were written in Arabic and Old Javanese. At the point when one adds to these the ever--growing number of YOGA Sutra interpretations, analyses, and studies right now being distributed in apparently every language on the planet (Japanese, Estonian, Turkish, and Polish, to give some examples), the image that rises is of something completely new: an Indian scriptural and philosophical custom that is really cosmopolitan, inserted in all aspects of the world, regardless of whether as of late rediscovered in the place where there is its introduction to the world. Be that as it may, before we go to these non--Indian appointments of the YOGA Sutra, we should initially arrange Patanjali's work and its unique Indian perusers in their old and medieval settings.

Chapter 2: Patanjali, the YOGA Sutra and Indian Philosophy

Now, it is important to present few pretty much untranslatable terms, remote concepts, and names of thinkers and philosophical schools that will return all through the remainder of this book: a cast of YOGA Sutra characters and ideas. Non specialist perusers not inspired by the arcana of Sanskrit phrasing might need to skirt quite a bit of this section.

The traditional Indian reporters saw the YOGA Sutra as a philosophical work, an examination concerning the connection among Spirit and Matter; a record of the functions of the brain and methods for realizing what is valid; an investigation of circumstances and logical results in the operations of the universe; and a manual for salvation. Just like the case with each significant Indian philosophical school and strict framework, these fields of request—philosophy (the nature of being), epistemology (knowing), psychology (the operations of the psyche), cosmology (the state of the universe), and soteriology (being spared)— are interwoven. While India has known many, numerous philosophical schools or frameworks (darshanas) in the course of the last three centuries, the accompanying six have been singled out, since the sixteenth century, as the "old style" Hindu darshanas: these are Samkhya, YOGA, Nyaya, Vaisheshika, Mimamsa, and Vedanta. The initial five of these can be gone back to the only remaining a very long time before the Common Era. Three among them—Nyaya ("Logic"), Vaisheshika ("Atomism"), and Mimamsa ("Vedic Exegesis")— are to a great extent unimportant to the historical backdrop of the YOGA Sutra and its history of understanding. Samkhya ("Enumeration"), the framework with which YOGA theory shares the most for all intents and purpose, is critical. The last, known as Vedanta—since it put together itself with respect to the way of thinking of the Upanishads, the last assortment of lessons inside the Vedic standard, which were otherwise called the "Veda's end" (veda--anta)—developed several hundreds of years after the fact. While there are three subschools of Vedanta reasoning—Dualist, Nondualist, and Qualified Nondualist—the Nondualist (Advaita) school that the extraordinary eighth--to ninth--century Shankaracharya (or Shankara) supported has been by a wide margin the most influential throughout the entire existence of Hindu idea, particularly in the course of the last 500 years. These Hindu frameworks didn't create in a vacuum in any case: two other philosophical frameworks that affected, and were impacted by, YOGA reasoning were those of early Jainism and Buddhism.

For the most part, one needs to start toward the start, yet as is so frequently the case with old Indian conventions, beginnings can be somewhat precarious. The YOGA Sutra is most likely not the primary Indian work to be given to either YOGA or YOGA, albeit Indian writings are famously hard to date. As a rule, Hindu sacred writings are comprehensively partitioned into Revelation (shruti, truly "that which was heard") and Tradition (smriti, literally "that which was reviewed"). The previous classification covers the Vedas, Brahmanas, Aranyakas, Upanishads, Dharmasutras, and the ceremonial Sutras, works considered to have been orally uncovered to the old diviners. As a rule, these works of Revelation date from between 1500 BCE and 400 CE. The last class contains India's two extraordinary sagas, the Mahabharata and Ramayana; the law books (called Smritis); and the Puranas and other partisan works called the Tan-tras and Agamas.

The most punctual surviving takes a shot at YOGA theory fall on the cusp between these two collections of sacred text. YOGA and Samkhya are examined at some length in the Katha Upanishad, a work of Revelation that probable dates from some time somewhere in the range of 300 and 100 BCE.

YOGA is likewise the chief focal point of the 6th book of another Upanishad, the Maitri, which may date from as late as or later than the YOGA Sutra. The Mahabharata contains broadened conversations of YOGA and YOGA in its 6th and twelfth books, the two of which are likewise more or then again less contemporary with the YOGA Sutra. A portion of the epic's previous books summon a lost YOGA custom that celebrated the apotheosis of the withering chariot warrior and his exemplified ascend to the universe of the divine beings: in its depictions of these courageous passings, the epic utilized "YOGA" to signify the sublime chariot that helped the warrior up through the circle of the sun to the raised plane of the awesome.

The part of the Mahabharata's 6th book wherein YOGA is a prime center is most popular under the name of the Bhagavad Gita, which contains a progression of lessons on human duty, love of God, and the "three YOGAs" of activity, information, and commitment as uncovered by the preeminent god Krishna to the epic warrior Arjuna. This work would turn into the establishment of YOGA as rehearsed by the different Vishnu-- revering (Vaishnava) customs, whose numerous advocates embedded parts on YOGA and YOGA into the Vaishnava Puranas. A few parts of the Mahabharata's twelfth book are additionally given to YOGA, together with Samkhya. In one of these, a heavenly figure named Hiranyagarbha ("Golden Embryo") is identified as both a maker god and the early stage revealer of the YOGA framework. Certain reporters give a title to his lessons: HiranyagarbhaYOGA- shastra ("Golden Embryo's Treatise on YOGA"); and a few sources statement or refer to his work, one of them widely. A few Puranas would likewise recognize Hiranyagarbha, instead of Patanjali, as the first revealer of YOGA. Notwithstanding, the greater part of the twelfth book's broad lessons on Samkhya and YOGA are ascribed to Yajnavalkya, an antiquated soothsayer with an Upanishadic family. Like Hiranyagarbha, Yajnavalkya is likewise recognized as the creator of various later takes a shot at YOGA and YOGA. As we will see in no time, the Puranas would altogether overlook Patanjali for these and other mythic YOGA diviners.

The Mahabharata's twelfth book additionally makes reference to an early gathering of Shiva--worshipping (Shaiva) religious zealots called the Pashupatas, who built up their own type of YOGA, called Pashupata YOGA, during a similar period.

Like the prior Katha Upanishad, the Mahabharata presents YOGA and Samkhya together. This is a typical of YOGA theory: that YOGA is nevertheless a minor departure from Samkhya reasoning, a program of reflection and different procedures raised upon an establishment of Samkhya mysticism. On the off chance that just thus, most YOGA Sutra original copies, in their colophons—the "credits" affixed to compositions in which dates, creators' and reporters' names, and other data are given—recognize the work as a "translation of Samkhya" (samkhya--pravachana). From the twelfth century ahead, creators would likewise allude to Patanjali's framework as "Samkhya with Ishvara" (seshvara samkhya), by method for saying that the YOGA framework's sole huge disparity from Samkhya hypothesis concerned "Ishvara."

Presently, on the off chance that YOGA theory were initially grounded in Samkhya, at that point one would hope to discover a primary work on Samkhya originating before the YOGA Sutra. This isn't the situation: the most punctual far reaching take a shot at Samkhya, the Samkhya Karika of Ishvara Krishna, is thought to date from a similar period as the YOGA Sutra.

Above all, few customs agree that an unbelievable sage named Kapila and his renowned understudies systematized Samkhya a few centuries before the start of the Common Era. The names of these sages are likewise found in the Mahabharata.

Eventually, the connection among Samkhya and YOGA—if without a doubt the two strands were ever independent from one another—is a chicken and egg question. What we cannot deny is that the hundreds of years preceding the start of the Common Era saw the development of almost the entirety of the incomparable Indian philosophical frameworks, frameworks of noteworthy modernity and unpredictability: Jainism, Buddhism, Nyaya, Vaisheshika, Mimamsa, YOGA, and Samkhya. Here, it is fundamental to comprehend that regardless of their stamped differences over issues of on-tology, soteriology, etc, the advocates of these schools—the creators of their primary writings and editorials—all conceded to a considerable number issues. Not the least of these was that a philosophical framework must be cognizant and thorough at each level. These philosophical frameworks were bound together Theories of Everything, and on the grounds that everything known to man is interconnected, everything—knowing, being, being spared, circumstances and logical results, time, space, mind, body, and so forth and so on.— must be reliable. Right now were particularly similar to the present Theory of Everything of current -day hypothetical material science, whose models for the starting point of the universe, the texture of room -time, the connection among issue and vitality, etc can't take into consideration the smallest defect or inner inconsistency. Something else, the ideal scientific gem breakdown.

Like current-day hypothetical physicists, the old reporters were individuals from a scholarly first class, composing for each other and not for the unwashed masses. They and their philosophical frameworks, did, nonetheless, contrast from those of present day hypothetical material science on two basic focuses. The first, and generally self-evident, is that their rationale behind decoding the functions of the universe was a soteriological one, completed for the sake of liberating people from the jail of enduring presence. This was a plan set in the main thousand years BCE, in both the Hindu Upanishads and the basic sacred texts of Buddhism and Jain-ism, the two exceptionally austere "new" religions of old India. As a result of their soteriological center, these schools created a dream of the universe, which, while completely unique in relation to our own, was nonethe-less level-headed, cognizant, and irrefutable based on their fundamental maxims. When of the YOGA Sutra, all of human information had been sorted out around this objective, to such an extent that every one of the main philosophical frameworks had the option to completely clarify and connect together totally known physical and profound marvels, including resurrection, recollections of previous existences, circumstances and logical results, "otherworldly" powers, etc into a bound together entirety.

Since, be that as it may, their clarifications for the concealed powers hidden the noticeable universe don't compare to those of current science, we moderns allude to their frameworks as mysticism, rather than the math-ematically provable laws of material science. This carries us to the subsequent significant purpose of contrast between the an-cient Indian logicians and current -day hypothetical physicists. The last use arithmetic, an all inclusive no-tation framework whose signifiers—numbers, conditions, calculations, etc—stay steady and trans-parently proportional to that which they connote, no mat-ter where or when that language is being composed or perused. Not so for the Indian logicians, whose language of articulation was Sanskrit, an "idealized" (this is the importance of the word) language no doubt, however a far less exact method of articulation than the language of science. This is the thing that made analyses so crucially important: so as to exhibit that the adages of a given philosophical framework were substantial, the specialized language of those maxims must be examined in hair--splitting point of interest. Consequently, analysts were likewise mindful to Indian hypotheses of language, of the intensity of words to speak to the real world—or even to (re)create reality, as on account of the Vedic mantras. In any case, this language--based design has made an-cient Indian way of thinking horribly delicate, mutable, and hard to get a handle on for current -day translators. As we saw for the basic meaning of YOGA in the last chap-ter, the interpretation of terms whose implications have changed after some time is an overwhelming errand. Supernatural places that were gone ahead in words as opposed to numerical recipes are more similar to lawful points of reference than the hypothesizes of hypothetical material science.

With this, let us harp for a minute on a portion of the essential standards of antiquated Samkhya--YOGA theory, which structure the setting for the greater part of the YOGA Sutra's truisms, just as their critiques. To start, this is a Dualist framework, involved Spirit and Matter. While there are numerous individual Persons or Spirits, Nature or Matter—which involves the entirety of the stuff of the universe, including each human body and each human brain—is one. In spite of the fact that it is bound together, our universe, the stuff of Prakriti, is in steady motion, transforming into a progression of twenty-four insecure elements, standards, or substrates, called tattvas. A portion of those are more steady than others, and the citta—which, since it is a piece of issue.— pulled and extended toward each path by the faculties, is continually arranging these into "me" (conscience, ahamkara), others, creatures, houses, and the various things on the planet. Absolutely discrete from these is Purusha, the twenty-fifth guideline.

For what reason is all of Nature continually in motion? It is here that we may perceive how Samkhya--YOGA, similar to each other Indian way of thinking, works in the administration of salvation, of liberating people from enduring presence. The objective here is to liberate the psyche from its misguided judgment that the Person or Spirit is caught in the pattern of death and resurrection. Albeit all the Persons known to mankind are installed in Matter, they are not dependent upon its laws: every Person is unadulterated, radiant, cognizance. However it is decisively when it comes into contact or vicinity with a Person (additionally called a "Watcher" or "Observer" [drastr])— that Nature (likewise called "What is Seen" [drsya]) is set into movement, advancing and declining into the different substrates of the wonderful world, putting on a scene for the Spectator to see. Despite the fact that Nature, including the psyche stuff, is completely oblivious—with its changes happening like the conduct of iron filings around a magnet—the incomparable Shankara's depiction of Nature as an on-screen character or an artist is one that numerous a logician has evoked as the centuries progressed. Indeed, even as Nature in its numerous stages is oblivious, its "execution" fills a need: to invigorate every Person, every "Onlooker," to understand that it's anything but a piece of the display it has been watching, that is, to understand its intrinsic "seclusion" (kaivalyam) from Her. At the point when this is practiced, She leaves the stage.

The job of the substrate that Patanjali calls the psyche-stuff is completely basic here, in light of the fact that it isn't just the quickest interface between the individual Person and the remainder of the universe, yet in addition the most unpredictable. These are the "turnings of thought" or "changes of the psyche-stuff" (citta--vritti) of the YOGA Sutra's definition of YOGA, which the reporter Vachaspati Mishra deciphered as "transformation into the type of an article." While the structure that that psychological transition will frequently take is that of the transient, passing loaded body with which it recognizes (by setting a self image), its latent capacity structures, characteristics, and augmentations are boundless. So it is that when the mind-stuff is drawn away from the body and the faculties and toward the unadulterated glowing cognizance of the Person, it apparently gets cognizant, while in certainty it is basically engrossing and mirroring the Person's own method of being.

In the Samkhya framework, the Person's continuous acknowledgment of its opportunity from the material world, demise and resurrection is affected through sound investigation into every one of the substrates through which Nature reverts, right down to net issue, the dormant stuff of the body and the universe. These incorporate the five components, the faculties, brain, and sense of self, finishing in the astuteness (buddhi). By completely knowing them, the Samkhya philosopher step by step comes to understand that the Person has no part in them. In YOGA, the technique for training changes to one of fixation, contemplation, and thoughtfulness, giving into a direct yogic observation (yogi--pratyaksha) of what genuinely is, a sort of information that is totally instinctive and nonconceptual, bypassing the "turnings of thought" completely. At the beginning, this includes controlling the exercises of the body, trailed by breath control, on the grounds that by stilling the breaths one calms the faculties and balances out the psyche. At that point, through extending phases of reflection, the practitioner's reasoning procedure or psyche -stuff is prepared away from the outward upgrades that typically render it so precarious and bound to the lower substrates of Matter, and afterward toward focus on the iridescent, stable Person itself. Since the brain -stuff retains and mirrors the characteristics of its undeniably unpretentious objects, it also turns out to be progressively inconspicuous, stable, and expansive. At the point when flawless fixation (samadhi) is accomplished, the mind-stuff gets unadulterated, peaceful, and straightforward to unadulterated awareness, extending out to the most remote compasses of room to vanish from see. With this, Nature has left the stage, and with nothing left to see, her Spectator, never again subject to the separating or twisting impacts of the mind-stuff, gets mindful of His detachment from the exercises of the material world, and "stays in His own structure." Once its disconnection from the motion of enduring presence has been acknowledged, enduring stops.

YOGA theory hypothesizes that the brain -stuff, or all the more appropriately, Nature's most elevated evolve, the keenness, has the ability to infiltrate anyplace and extend interminably. This was a subject of supported conversation in the old style commentarial custom, and its suggestions keep on reverberating in insightful circles down to the current day. Here it is basic to take note of a significant qualification between old style Indian and current Western speculations of discernment.

The equivalent consistently applies to the elements of the apparent article, with the end goal that when the reasoning rule or acumen is watching the furthest and most unobtrusive ranges of the universe, it is all the while loosened up to widespread measurements.

This rule, as of now presented in the Mahabharata, is conveyed forward in a wide assortment of chips away at YOGA. The suggestion here is that a yogi's body achieves widespread measurements also: this is one of the heavenly powers of the yogi insinuated in the YOGA Sutra's third section.

When it has been prepared through the act of yogic contemplation, the brain -stuff 's boundless potential for extension makes way for what are frequently alluded to as the "heavenly powers," the fundamental subject of the YOGA Sutra's third part. These incorporate the psyche stuff 's capacity to go into the collections of different creatures, the intensity of flight, imperceptibility, the capacity to guess others' thoughts, to know one's past and future lives, and information on what is unpretentious, covered up, and removed. Colophons allude to this as the part on vibhuti, a word that truly signifies "the ability to broaden every-where." When comprehended with regards to Samkhya--YOGA mysticism, there is nothing extraordinary about these forces. As the brain -stuff assimilates and mirrors the Person's glowing intensity of awareness, it, similar to cognizance, gets ubiquitous, equipped for entering or changing into anything, and perceptive of everything.

While the entirety of the significant Indian philosophical frameworks have salvation as their objective, and keeping in mind that most concur that the activities of the brain are both the source and the potential answer for the issue of affliction, they take profoundly various situations on a few fundamental focuses. Since we will be coming back to it much of the time in these pages, one of these—the relationship of the Per- child (Purusha), or Self (Atman, Brahman) to the material world—must be tended to here. As we have seen, in the Dualist arrangement of Samkhya--YOGA, both individual Persons (Purushas) and the Matter where they are installed are genuine, yet they are drastically independent. Here, the objective of training is to understand their separateness and in this manner free the Person from its envisioned traps with the material world. In differentiation to this, the Nondualist arrangement of Advaita Vedanta keeps up that the widespread Self (Brahman) is genuine however that the material world is stunning. There is nothing that exists that isn't the Self; be that as it may, because of "inestimable dream" (maya), singular selves accept that they are particular substances, cut off from each other and the general Self by deceptive bodies and the stuff of the world. Here the objective of training is to understand that all that isn't Brahman is a dream. By genuinely realizing that everything is one and inner to Brahman, the individual self accomplishes personality with the general Self, despite the fact that in all actuality it never was genuinely particular from it. At long last, as indicated by the Buddha's lessons, both the individual self and the material world are incredible, and there is no otherworldly Self. There is just misery, which the "no--self " (anatta) relates to, because of the wanderings of the psyche, which pursues illusory items that are its own projections.

This is all strong stuff, abundant observer to the way that the perspective of Patanjali and his old style pundits was altogether different from our own. For this, the profoundly specialized philosophical entries of these works are regularly scattered with implications to genuine -world phe-nomena that are undeniably increasingly natural. We have just noticed Shankara's examination of Prakriti to an entertainer or artist who puts on an act for Purusha, her detached Spectator. Along these lines, as well, the analogy of a magnet and iron filings to inspire the impact of cognizant Spirit on uncon-scious Matter is one that doesn't give us cerebrum cramps. A few pictures are very dazzling: the impression of a blossom in a glass, water sliding through the floodgate door of a water system channel, honey bees following their sovereign, a humble wooden truck conveying a valuable, fragrant heap of saffron. Strikingly missing from the YOGA Sutra and its discourses is the smallest reference to a yogic "way of life," of living in concordance with nature in a backwoods presence or remote religious community, isolation, or cavern.

Where one would hope to discover such references is the most clear and user--friendly bit of the YOGA Sutra, the second of its four parts (padas), which is dedicated to rehearse. Here, two sorts of training are proposed. For the nonspecialist, there is "useful YOGA" (kriya YOGA), which has three sections: parsimony, the investigation and recitation of consecrated songs and syllables, and commitment to Ishvara. For the specialist questing for freedom from enduring presence, Patanjali presents the eight-part practice, which includes the (1) inward and (2) external restrictions, (3) act, (4) breath control, (5) withdrawal of the faculties, (6) obsession, (7) reflection, and (8) unadulterated consideration. Containing the last twenty-eight sections of part 2 and the three opening stanzas of part 3, Patanjali's introduction of the eight-section practice is a short reprieve from the exceptionally hypothetical focal point of the more noteworthy majority of his work. A conservative bit by bit way to deal with the act of reflection, it gets restricted consideration from the traditional observers. There are two potential clarifications for this general commentarial dismissal for training. The first is that the reporters didn't ruminate or rehearse YOGA. The second is that despite the fact that they may have attempted the eight--part practice in their private lives, their open jobs as pundits obliged them to remain on message and to concentrate on the YOGA Sutra as a Theory of Everything.

Standing (or sitting in lotus pose) at the oppo-site end of the range are the current YOGA masters, who, in their continuous references to the YOGA Sutra, infrequently allude to any however the thirty--one refrains that contain Patanjali's instructing on the eight-section practice. In this manner they frequently mistake the part for the entire, introducing the eight-section practice as the "es-sence" of YOGA, to the rejection of the work's other 164 refrains. A similar YOGA masters, just as some basic YOGA researchers, additionally will in general accept that Patanjali by and by rehearsed the YOGA portrayed in the YOGA Sutra, that he was something in excess of a scholarly creator of a Theory of Everything.

The issue of the verifiable Patanjali and his relationship to the work credited to him takes us back to the subject of roots. As I have just noticed, a few YOGAs were stylish before the creation of the YOGA Sutra, and a portion of these included contemplation. What's more, there were a few reflection customs—those of the Jains and Buddhists specifically—that while they didn't call themselves "YOGA" unquestionably foreseen a considerable lot of the ideas and practices found in Patanjali's work. So it is that some old style observers and most basic researchers have seen Patanjali not as a unique creator, but instead as a compiler who wove together in any event two—yet maybe upwards of six—previous YOGA customs or writings.

Lord Bhoja, a significant eleventh--century pundit, was

simply the first to concern—fundamentally for motivations behind self--promotion—with the character, or various personalities, of Patanjali. "Patanjali" is recorded as the name of one of the twenty--six legendary Divine Serpents in various Puranas. One of these was the 6th century Vishnudharmottara Purana, a work from Kashmir, where Patanjali has for quite some time been especially respected. As per the Vishnudharmottara, "the picture of Patanjali's YOGA educating ought to have the type of Ananta," Ananta being the name of the celestial Lord of Serpents who bears the whole universe upon his thousand extended cobra hoods.

Chapter 3: How YOGA Sutra was Discovered in the West

In contrast to the YOGA Sutra's old style observers, moderately hardly any cutting edge YOGA researchers are either Indian or Hindu. In the course of the last one hundred years specifically, remote researchers have created the main part of the new hypothetical points of view on Patanjali's work. The narrative of how outside researchers supported into or, all the more appropriately, resuscitated the YOGA Sutra's antiquated conventions is as entrancing and implausible as the weird multi year conflict of societies normally known as the British Raj. At some point in the late eighteenth century, a portion of the British who had been adequately controlling a great part of the rich region of Bengal for quite a few years were starting to understand that outside occupation could have unexpected outcomes.

Things had started swimmingly enough on June 23, 1757, when, amidst the Seven Years' War, a multitude of three thousand men drove by the British colonel Robert Clive had crushed the Nawab of Bengal at the Battle of Plassey. This was a defining moment in the development of what might turn into the British Empire in India, yet now, England's impact in India was roundabout. Going about as an intermediary for the Crown in eighteenth-century. India was the British East India Company, an exchanging consortium that was nevertheless one among a few adversary organizations competing for command over the tremendous assets and markets of Asia.

In Bengal, the Company's most noteworthy rival was its French homologue, the French East India Company. Warren Hastings, picked Calcutta (today known as Kolkata), at the time minimal in excess of a swampy town of mud cabins, to be its capital. The Company was above all else a business venture, whose raison d'être was to expand benefits for its investors. To this end it enrolled exceptionally youngsters from Britain (their normal age was sixteen) to direct its gigantic estates and industrial facility tasks, which were controlled by nearby subcontractors.

A significant number of these youngsters ended up being self--serving swashbucklers, with the individuals who succeeded coming back to Britain a few years after the fact with tremendous individual fortunes. Pre-work preparing was not a high need in those early years: so as to be employed, a declaration in bookkeeping was adequate, and all other preparing—in nearby dialects, business organization, etc—was of the on--the--work assortment. In any case, the common organization of the Company's domains incorporated the organization of equity, and it was here that a statement in Hastings' Judicial Plan of 1772 gave rise, yet in a roundabout way, to the British "revelation" of the YOGA Sutra. That proviso declared that instead of forcing British customary law upon the individuals of Bengal, which would have been frightfully out of line but not unprecedented, Hindus would be decided by Hindu law and Muslims as indicated by Islamic law.

Shockingly for the British, they had no information on either. Islamic law was a generally simple fix; since it had been the law of the Mughal Empire in India for decades, its ordinance, regardless of whether it was written in Arabic and Persian, was at any rate recognizable. Hindu law, be that as it may, a was obscure area. What were the codes of Hindu law, and where were they to be found? From the start, it was resolved that the wellsprings of Hindu law could all the more effectively be uncovered of Hindu law books than by watching and recording contemporary nearby traditions. As the British were made to comprehend by the brahmin strict masters known as pandits, the ordinance of Hindu law had been written in the language known as Sanskrit, the "consummated" language of their sacred texts. Thus, it was that in the last decades of the eighteenth century an unexpected result of the British control of Bengal was the pressing need to learn Sanskrit, one of the most confoundedly troublesome dialects on earth.

In the most punctual periods of their expectation to absorb information, the British were totally subject to the Bengali pandits, whom Hastings effectively selected for opening the puzzles of everything Hindu. They distinguished the essential lessons of sacrosanct Hindu law (Dharma Shastra, abbreviated to "the Shaster" by the British), and they deciphered them and deciphered their significance to the British, by and large through the mechanism of Bengali, the communicated in language of the region. At last, the culmination of that errand would tumble to a Sanskritist named Henry Thomas Colebrooke. Together with Jones, Colebrooke was an establishing father of British Orientalism, and their disclosure and steady dominance of a significant number of the marvels of the Sanskrit language and its enormous scholarly custom might be seen as an immediate and glad symptom of Hastings' Judicial Plan. Jones, a far off precursor of Lady Di, had first shown up in Kolkata in March of 1783. Sent there to fill in as equity on the Supreme Court of Bengal, he was a strange appointed authority in light of the fact that he had, long preceding examining law in the mid 1770s, separated himself as an expert of old dialects.

Not long after taking his post, notwithstanding, Jones started to presume that the nearby pandits had maybe been snookering him and his col-leagues, making up lawful decisions on the fly or to further their own potential benefit even as they professed to cite part and section of the Shaster. He said as much in a letter kept in touch with Hastings in 1784, however his proper task for a Digest of Hindu Law on Contracts and Successions would not be submitted until 1788. In contrast to the 1776 Code, the summary would be an "in--house" interpretation, completely arranged this time by British Sanskritists. Jones and his kindred individuals from the Asiatic Society brazenly alluded to themselves as Orientalists, a term that has been related, in the wake of Edward Said's weighty Orientalism (1978), with majestic control, provincial ventures, and the ideas of European predominance typified in Kipling's "White man's burden." Such charges are out and out legitimate for the Anglicists, whose speculations of "Oriental unreasonableness" came to rule Britain's inexorably radical approaches toward India from the 1830s forward. In any case, as Rosane Rocher and others have illustrated, the demeanor of the Orientalists, the Company's researcher -administrators of the early decades of the nineteenth century, was different.

Colebrooke's 1823-27 examination is a model of economy and lucidity, strikingly extensive in both degree and profundity. In it, Colebrooke demonstrates himself to be profoundly thoughtful to Indian way of thinking, as he presents the frameworks in a goal and fair way. With a solitary special case, he shows extraordinary regard for his subject, permitting now and again that India may have been the wellspring of a few old Greek philosophical principles. This was nevertheless one part of his more extensive vision of the historical backdrop of human idea. At his debut discourse to the Royal Asiatic Society of Great Britain and Ireland, introduced on March 15, 1823, he straight stated that all of human progress had its starting point in Asia, for which the West owed that landmass an obligation of appreciation. Here, he was essentially repeating the situation of the British Orientalists, and keeping in mind that the facts demonstrate that the voices of the Orientalists would before long be overwhelmed by those of the jingoist Anglicists who won the day as far as British approach, their valuation for everything Indian would in later decades be raised to a matter of confidence among the European Romantics, who saw old India as the lost heaven of mankind and the source of all human intelligence and otherworldliness. This ruddy vision would bit by bit transform into a progressively solid good news of Indian exceptionalism, whose topics possibly found in the compositions and lessons of the Theosophical Society, Swami Vivekananda, and present day - day Hindu patriots.

Colebrooke's investigation of the six frameworks seems to have been solely founded on his own thorough investigation of Sanskrit-language original copies, attempted without plan of action to the Indian pandits. (As we will see, his own assortment of such original copies was unbelievable.) Colebrooke's 1823 examination, far shorter than those he would later distribute on Nyaya--Vaisheshika and Mimamsa--Vedanta, isn't titled "Samkhya--YOGA," but instead essentially "Samkhya." Colebrooke clarifies the oversight of "YOGA" from his title by contending that YOGA is nevertheless a variation type of Samkhya reasoning. Right now, basically following the commentarial custom referenced in the last part, which talks about YOGA as just "Samkhya with Ishvara" (seshvara samkhya)— with Ishvara, the "Ace" of YOGA, interpreted by numerous analysts as meaning "God."

Colebrooke harps however little on the peculiarity of the YOGA school, giving less than five pages of his investigation (contrasted with the twenty--eight offered over to Samkhya) to its principles, observers, and traditions. One may trait this apparently pretentious mentality as essentially spilling out of the way that the YOGA Sutra is regularly called an "understanding of Samkhya" (samkhya--pravachana) in its original copy colophons. Noticing this, Colebrooke decided to concentrate on the essential wellspring of Samkhya reasoning, the Samkhya Karika, which he ascribed to Kapila, the unbelievable organizer of the school, as opposed to its creator Ishvara Krishna.

While plainly Colebrooke isn't excited by the statutes of Samkhya theory, he in any case acknowledges it as reasoning. Similar holds for his records of the four different schools, for which his general demeanor of regard far exceeds the infrequent trashing comment. In his whole investigation of the six frameworks, the sole examples wherein Colebrooke utilizes "over the top" or utilizes some other such stacked term are those cited here on the subject of the YOGA Sutra. His selection of words would keep on reverberating through- out a significant part of the nineteenth century.

The American Orientalist Fitzedward Hall was of a somewhat more grounded feeling, as confirm in an 1859 production with the unfortunate title A Contribution to- wards an Index to the Bibliography of the Indian Philosophical Systems. Note, in any case, that Hall's analysis is coordinated against the whole group of YOGA theory.

Rajendralal Mitra, who cites Hall in the prologue to his 1883 interpretation of the YOGA Sutra, next makes a move that would be broadly followed for a significant part of the next century: he isolates YOGA theory from India's yogis, putting the onus of the over the top not on the YOGA Sutra itself yet rather on its maltreatment by its alleged professionals.

While the YOGA Sutra has been called numerous things by numerous individuals, over the top isn't the primary that rings a bell. Why, at that point, so much solid and fierceness in regards to India's over the top yogis? The vast majority of us in the twenty-- first century see India's conventional yogis as serene, woodland abiding sages, living in agreement with winged creature and monster and spending their days and evenings in riveted reflection on the Absolute inside. This is the manner by which the woods sages are depicted in India's antiquated writing, and in that immortal place where there is perpetual convention, that is the manner by which they have remained. While these people are no place alluded to as yogis in the antiquated writing, the YOGA Sutra and different works from the early hundreds of years CE (the Hindu Bhagavad Gita and Maitri Upanishad and the Buddhist Miliandapanha, for instance) do; in them, just because, experts of the different kinds of YOGA they embrace are designated "yogis."

How fascinating, at that point, that not a solitary nineteenth-- century account, by either Europeans or Indians—or by the yogis themselves—depicts them as quiet religious zealots rehearsing reflection pace the YOGA Sutra. In- stead, the dominant part of records from the sixteenth century ahead portray yogis as either homeless people or ragtag soldier of fortune warriors. On the first † tally, a huge number of observer reports talk about ravaging groups of yogis acting like shake--down craftsmen, mobbing passageways to sanctuaries, journey destinations, and open markets, arranging monstrosity appears (the "mango stunt" and notorious beds of nails), or basically causing an uproar until annoyed dealers would take care of them essentially to leave and hector another person. On the second, they were seen similarly as the modern-day Taliban, as part strict aficionado and part fear based oppressor, battling groups of warriors known to harm their adversaries or slice their throats to drink their warm blood.

This was the Europeans' outcast perspective on India's

yogis. Be that as it may, what do insider Indian records let us know? In the medieval sacred writings known as the Tantras, the term yogi regularly alluded to a Tantric authority who had gotten different commencements that engaged him to rehearse Tantric YOGA, which required, in addition to other things, the ability to take over others' bodies and to associate explicitly with savage female predators called Yoginis. Burden to the unenlightened who may endeavor the equivalent, be that as it may: the Yoginis would destroy them and eat them, which unquestionably puts another wrinkle on the "Yogini" Gonika of Iyengar folklore. In quite a bit of India's medieval and present day dream and experience writing, the insidious miscreant is known as a yogi, and even today, when shrewd kids won't rest around evening time, their folks will compromise that "the yogi will come and remove you." Regarded with fear and dread by the Hindu people, India's yogis state that their heavenly powers stream straightforwardly from enabling inceptions and remarkable accomplishments of self-control. However, while these forces regularly line up with those depicted in the YOGA Sutra's third part, not many Tantric schools or orders have ever expressly connected their hypothesis or practice to Patanjali's heritage.

Having said this, there is likely increasingly behind Colebrooke's references to the "over the top" than basically a philosophical aversion for a reprobate way of life. Here, a nineteenth-century assortment of legends, gathered by a yogi having a place with the ground-breaking request known as the Kanphata Yogis ("Split--Eared Yogis") or Nath Yogis ("Yogi Lords"), is profoundly enlightening. In it, we read of a verifiable figure named Mastnath whose numerous heavenly accomplishments remembered calling down diseases for towns that would not offer him contributions, transforming camel bones into gold, and raising an attacked ruler named Man Singh to the royal position of the realm of Marwar in the current western Indian territory of Rajasthan. Right now, Mastnath delivered a progression of supernatural occurrences finishing in the abrupt demise of the youthful sovereign's adversary, as a byproduct of which the Yogi Lords were conceded a system of sanctuaries and religious communities all through the realm. James Tod, a Company specialist, likewise chronicled the equivalent wild part in Marwar history, however he put a through and through various turn on things. At the end of the day, a Yogi Lord had penetrated the adversary camp and killed its pioneer.

All through the last three decades of the eighteenth century, the Company had wound up set in opposition to a yogi rebellion in Bengal. For a great part of the eighteenth century, the Company likewise ended up countered by the yogis in its endeavors to control and adventure north Indian business.

In the years around 1795, Colebrooke was working in the Company's utilize at Mirzapur. At this point a cultivated Sanskritist, he no uncertainty made a trip downriver to the heavenly city of Varanasi—which was around then amidst a monetary and strict renaissance—for access to Sanskrit compositions to add to his developing assortment. There, the incredible western Indian exchanging places of Sindhia and Holkar were benefactors of a traditionalist brand of

Hinduism, which they cultivated by setting up brahmin "universities" for the preparation of pandits. The arrangement worked so well that by 1810 there were in excess of 40,000 brahmins living on good cause there, representing almost 20 percent of the city's complete populace. Be that as it may, the yogis were additionally an important nearness. The 1827–28 evaluation information demonstrate that "Hindu Fakirs"— that is, yogis—made up 4 percent of the city's whole populace, however this just alluded to individuals from the homeless person orders living there for all time, instead of the crowds of vagrant yogis that were continually going through.

With the Sanyasi and Fakir Rebellion an ongoing memory in Bengal, and the profoundly unmistakable nearness of meandering religious zealots in Varanasi and Mirzapur a contrasting reality, Colebrooke would have been by and large acquainted with the yogis and their "over the top" ways. Given that none of these yogis had any intrigue at all in the philosophical and thoughtful lessons of the YOGA Sutra, one must ask whether there stayed some other gathering from Indian society that had kept on developing its antiquated conventions. The conspicuous up-and-comer would have been the pandits, the experts of the brahmin schools—of Varanasi in the Gangetic heartland and Nadia in Bengal—whose stock in exchange was the transmission of conventional Hindu information from age to age.

Before we leave Colebrooke and his concise, ominous perusing of the YOGA Sutra behind, we need likewise to consider two quantifiable information sources to which the incomparable Orientalist would not have been unconcerned. All through his investigation of the six frameworks, Colebrooke makes reference to the commentarial customs of each separate school, taking note of the "countless" takes a shot at Nyaya and Vedanta specifically. Truth be told, be- tween 100 and 1660 CE, no less than 511 discourses and subcommentaries were composed on the Nyaya and Vaisheshika Sutras alone. For a similar period, just twelve discourses and subcommentaries were composed on the YOGA Sutra—and of these, none, except for Bhoja's "Illustrious Sun," can be said to have been made by an advocate out of Patanjali's framework. At base, there never was, appropriately, a "YOGA School" of reasoning. Between Vijnanabhikshu's two sixteenth--century works and Colebrooke's time, just seven analyses were composed on the YOGA Sutra. Of these, two were Jain, and the other five, made by writers living and writing in south India, by and large subverted, instead of clarified, its YOGA lessons. Perusing Patanjali's work through the viewpoint of Vedanta and Hindu reverential devotion, they were, basically, disassembling it. Outside of these, lone a sprinkling of writers even alluded to the YOGA Sutra in their works. These information lead one to presume that by the sixteenth or seventeenth century Patanjali's YOGA framework had to a great extent become the surrendered stepchild of Indian way of thinking.

Another kind of metric further backings these ends. Colebrooke was a pioneer in the assortment of Indian compositions, which were the sole information hotspot for composed conventions in precolonial India. Aside from original copies of the YOGA Sutra, the oral conventions of India's yogis and pandits would have been the sole living connects to YOGA reasoning, and as we have seen, these too had obviously vanished by Colebrooke's time. This might not have upset him especially, since as a man of letters, he would have felt increasingly comfortable with original copies, thus he was.

Colebrooke's assortment of YOGA Sutra compositions was little in contrast with those speaking to the next five schools. I would contend that as much as any authentic reproduction of impacts, transmissions, heredities, oral customs, etc, such a quantitative appraisal is, for the period we are taking a gander at—that of the primary contact between European Sanskritists and Indian philosophical works in Sanskrit—the most exact information source that one may attract upon to reproduce the wide layouts of the Indian philosophical scene. Remembering the moderately short life expectancies of original copies in most south Asian atmospheres, surviving composition assortments offer windows into which writings recorders were duplicating at the command of their supporters from, much of the time, no sooner than the seventeenth century. As a rule, those supporters would have been sovereignty, individuals from the gentry, well off dealers, brahmin pandits, and sanctuary and devout organizations. These were the significant wellsprings of the composition assortments that European Orientalists started to accumulate in the nineteenth century, thus they can furnish us with a quantitative assessment of the general significance of the different schools.

Having said this, we should ask whether similar extents would hold up if we somehow happened to take a gander at a more extensive testing (with inspecting numbers being conversely corresponding to safety buffers).

For each composition on YOGA theory appropriate (barring Hatha and Tantric YOGA) held in significant Indian original copy libraries and files, there exist about forty Vedanta compositions and almost the same number of Nyaya-- Vaisheshika compositions. Original copies of the YOGA Sutra and its analyses represent only one--third of all compositions on YOGA reasoning, the other 66% being dedicated chiefly to Hatha and Tantric YOGA. Be that as it may, it is the figure of 1.27 percent that hangs out in most elevated help, since it discloses to us that after the late sixteenth century for all intents and purposes nobody was replicating the YOGA Sutra in light of the fact that nobody was authorizing YOGA Sutra original copies, and nobody was appointing YOGA Sutra compositions on the grounds that nobody was keen on perusing the YOGA Sutra. Some have contended that guidance in the YOGA Sutra depended on repetition remembrance or reciting: this is the situation of Krishnamacharya's biographers just as of various basic researchers. However, this is unadulterated hypothesis, undercut by the nineteenth--century perceptions of James Ballantyne, Dayananda Saraswati, Rajendralal Mitra, Friedrich Max Müller, and others. There is no express record, in either the commentarial custom itself or in the sacrosanct or mainstream written works of the previous 2,000 years, of followers of the YOGA school retaining, reciting, or guaranteeing an oral transmission for their conventions.

Given these information, we may presume that Colebrooke's curt, if not threatening, treatment of the YOGA Sutra without a doubt originated from the way that by his time, Patanjali's framework had become a vacant signifier, with no conventional schoolmen to elucidate or guard it and no formal or casual outlets of guidance in its lessons. It had become a dying convention, an object of all inclusive lack of interest. The YOGA Sutra had in every way that really matters been lost until Colebrooke discovered it.

Chapter 4: Your Perception determines Your Belief System: The Cosmic Drama

"Discernment is the truth" is an aphorism comprehended by marketing experts and advertisement administrators. They get that—exact or not—what we see to be genuine decides our reactions. Envision strolling into a faintly lit room. As we glance around, we notice a looped shape in a corner. A snake! Our heart thumps quicker. Breathing gets fomented. Adrenaline fills the circulation system. Our psyche quickly looks for the best possible game-plan: Should we run, call 911, shout for help? Dread based musings more than once intrude on reason: What if it's harmful and I get chomped? Who will think about my youngsters in the event that I pass on! At that point, intuitively, we go after the light switch. Light has the ability to dis-close the puzzles composed by shadows. There is no snake; there never was. What we thought was a snake was only a curled bit of rope. Despite the fact that we were never in any peril, by dishonestly seeing the rope for a snake, we encountered similar considerations, physiological reactions, and activities as though it were a snake. Our view of the snaked rope in the diminish light became—for some time—our existence.

Discernments become the premise of conviction frameworks, and conviction frameworks, paying little mind to how inconspicuous and refined, resemble channels that permit certain bits of data to go through while blocking others. We may accept that an adoring, lenient God exists, that human instinct is inherently acceptable, that the reason forever is to serve others, that blessed messengers exist, that the strategies of our own ideological group are best for the nation, that an apple daily fends the specialist off, that excellence is its own prize, and that better to save up for a rainy day. Yet, what components of truth may these convictions channel? Are these convictions just somewhat evident? Would they be able to be totally bogus? What number of snaked ropes does our conviction framework contain?

Analyze the "real factors" that characterize your life. How have presumptions, past encounters, expectations, and fears shaped your universe? Do you see a merciless world, or does life take after a bowl of fruits? A futile way of life or a luxurious situation? Is the world a risky spot or a Garden of Eden? On the off chance that you get up each morning to find that you are amidst a futile way of life, huge hurrying rodents will populate your reality. It follows that in the event that you see the planet as gagged with vicious exercises, it will be essential for you to "pay special mind to Number One" and watch your back. Life will be a distressing encounter. Then again, on the off chance that you see a Garden of Eden outside your window, happiness and bliss will encompass you.

For the greater part of us, life includes swinging from a proportion of satisfaction and security to misery, fretfulness, and dread. Our experience of life relies upon how we see the happenings existing apart from everything else. On the off chance that everything is by all accounts continuing as per our arrangements, we see daylight and paradise; if our arrangements don't occur to coordinate what life permits, presence can take on shocking tones.

Swinging to and fro from magnificent to shocking encounters is itself a wellspring of anguish. We stick to pleasurable encounters while attempting to get away from agonizing ones. The individuals who feel worn out on the persevering and eccentric good and bad times of life contain most of profound searchers. Others are attracted to profound life since they are disappointed or frustrated with probably some part of life. Notwithstanding the particular reasons, the initial moves toward otherworldly life are regularly spurred by some proportion of discontent, instability, or eagerness.

Prickly inquiries follow this disturbance: Is there something more to life? Something more profound and all the more satisfying? What is the genuine idea of life, and is there any reason or significance to it? Do we need to endure? For what reason would we say we are conceived? How and where does God fit into the entirety of this? Does God by any chance exist?

The responses to these inquiries—and the sky is the limit from there—can be found in the YOGA Sutras.

The lessons and practices of the YOGA Sutras depend on three standards:

- Suffering isn't brought about by powers outside of us however by a broken and restricted view of life and of what our identity is. Our fundamental misperception offers ascend to unlimited yearnings for sense fulfillment. Since everything known to man is continually changing, nothing in

- Nature is equipped for bringing enduring satisfaction.
- The steadfast harmony we look for is acknowledged by encountering the boundless and endless Peace that is our True Identity. In spite of the fact that clouded by numbness, it exists inside us, holding on to be uncovered. This experience is edification—Self-acknowledgment.
- Self-acknowledgment is accomplished by acing the brain. Similarly, as just a perfect, undistorted mirror can mirror our face as it genuinely seems to be, just a one-pointed and peaceful brain can part the shroud of obliviousness to uncover and mirror the Self.

The push to liberate the brain from the confinements of obliviousness is a show that has been rehashed since days of yore. The establishment of this dramatization is outlined in three fundamental statutes: Purusha, Prakriti, and Avidya.

Purusha: Pure Unbounded Consciousness

The experience of the Purusha as our True Identity is illumination or Self-acknowledgment. The immediate experience of the Purusha gives a definitive mission.

Much, despite the fact that not all, of the YOGA Sutras depends on the Sankhya theory. Sankhya recommends that there are a limitless number of isolated Purushas, all being ubiquitous and omniscient. However during Sri Patanjali's time, there existed other philosophical schools that utilized the term Purusha to assign One Absolute Truth or Self. The YOGA Sutras go separate ways with Sankhya at a few key focuses and the sutras themselves offer no immediate motivation to accept that Sri Patanjali held to the multi-Purusha rule.

Prakriti: Undifferentiated Matter

Prakriti is the setting for this epic. Because of numbness, Prakriti may some of the time appear to carry on like an obstruction, darkening our experience of the Purusha. In actuality, it gives us the difficulties and exercises that lead to Self-acknowledgment. In doing as such, Prakriti assists with revealing our concealed qualities and shortcomings.

Avidya: Spiritual Ignorance

Each saint has a shortcoming: Superman has kryptonite; Achilles, his heel. Right now, numbness, deters the experience of our True Identity. It is the essential disarray of the Seer (Purusha) with the seen (Prakriti): seeing the fleeting as perpetual, the polluted as unadulterated, the difficult as wonderful, and the non-Self as the Self. Avidya is the reason for anguish. Also, the lessons of YOGA direct the path toward its evacuation.

The main component missing right now a legend or courageous woman. That job has a place with you. What's more, there is no preferred manual over the

YOGA Sutras.

In Sri Patanjali's day, it was regular for lessons, including consecrated writings, to be saved and transmitted orally. Those lessons, which for quite a long time have been passed down from ace to teach, are the premise of the content you grasp today. We don't have a clue when or by whom the sutras originally made the progress to composed structure.

"Words usually can't do a picture justice." So is every sutra. The most valuable system to utilize when considering the YOGA Sutras is to move toward them as you would a bit of workmanship or verse, where an exacting, there-is-only-single direction to-comprehend this viewpoint can cover the subtleties, magnificence, and different degrees of significance. The YOGA Sutras can be analyzed and delighted in from numerous edges, every feature uncovering another part of truth. You will find more degrees of importance for yourself as you proceed with your investigation and practice.

The YOGA Sutras are additionally normally known as Raja YOGA, the Royal YOGA. They earned this honorable status since they present otherworldliness as a comprehensive science, all around pertinent to individuals of all confidence customs. These are lessons that are alive, that reverberate at the degree of our inward soul, arousing recollections of our True Identity. The rules and practices of Raja YOGA bring the accomplishment of otherworldly illumination inside the compass of anybody through a handy bit by bit process established, in actuality, experience.

Sri Patanjali

Insights about Sri Patanjali's life are sparse. It is accepted that he was conceived at some point between 5000 BCE and 300 CE, with numerous cutting edge researchers setting his introduction to the world at some point in the second century BCE. He may have been one individual or a few with a similar name. Some state he was a doctor, legal advisor, or a grammarian. Perhaps he was each of the three. Absolutely, by analyzing the YOGA Sutras, we can witness the mentality of an all encompassing doctor, a keen lawful psyche goal on shutting the escape clauses in his introduction, and an ace of succinct language. Despite the fact that Sri Patanjali is known as the "Father of YOGA," he didn't make it. The basic lessons are old to such an extent that nobody knows for certain when they began. Sri Patanjali is the "Father of YOGA" since he was an amazing instructor who obviously saw the reason for affliction and had the option to recommend a pragmatic bit by bit way out of it. In spite of the fact that the YOGA Sutras are loaded up with superb philosophical bits of knowledge and disclosures, his expectation never wanders from the down to earth. Sri Patanjali always remembers that hypothesis without training will never genuinely fulfill us—and it is right now can discover proof of his extraordinary empathy. Just somebody who completely feels for the enduring that goes to profound numbness would be so resolutely decided in calling attention to the way to opportunity. Sri Patanjali doesn't need us to while away our time appreciating stunning philosophical bits of knowledge. His aim is to assist us with excursion of obliviousness as fast as could be expected under the circumstances.

A few stories of Sri Patanjali's introduction to the world have endure the hundreds of years. As indicated by one legend, Sri Patanjali was the grandson of Lord Brahma—maker of the universe. Another story gives us the starting point of his name. Right now, Patanjali is the manifestation of Ananta, the thousand-headed snake. Ananta (lit., the unbounded) is the watchman of the shrouded treasures—the sacrosanct lessons—of the earth. Ananta likewise fills in as the lounge chair whereupon Lord Vishnu—the type of God as preserver—rests before the start of creation. Ananta himself is additionally viewed as a manifestation of Lord Vishnu.

Ananta wanted to carry the yogic lessons to earth, yet he expected to take birth in the belly of a righteous lady to do as such. His inquiry finished with Gonika, who was an incredible yogini (a female expert of YOGA) and who had been appealing to God for a child commendable enough to get the information on YOGA. One morning, while occupied with venerate, she offered to the Lord the main thing she had—a bunch of water. She respectfully lifted the water into her measured palms. Similarly as she was going to make the contribution, she saw a modest snake swimming in the little pool of water in her grasp. Her awe expanded as the little snake type of Ananta accepted full human structure. He prostrated before her and inquired as to whether she would acknowledge him as her child with the goal that he could carry the incredible study of YOGA to mankind. Gonika gladly concurred and named her awesome child Patanjali: a contribution (anjali) who fell (pat) from paradise.

Sri Patanjali is regularly portrayed as half human and half snake, with his four-equipped human middle rising up out of the curls of his snake lower half. Two of his hands are as one before his chest in respectful welcome, a signal that is alluded to as an anjali. At the point when given by a sage or God, this signal reflects both a welcome and a gift. One upraised hand holds the chakra, or plate, which symbolizes the turning wheel of time and the law of circumstances and logical results. His other inspired hand holds the conch, representative of the vitality of the early stage sound, OM. This calls his understudies to rehearse and reports that the world as they probably are aware it will be changed.

Sri Patanjali presents the objective of YOGA—our goal—in sutra two of this segment. Where we are currently—stuck in a misperception of our True Identity—is tended to by sutra three and a few sutras dispersed all through the content. You will likewise discover portrayals of the different mental alterations that shading the psyche, a few reflection procedures, and commonsense clues for picking up and keeping up undisturbed serenity of brain.

Chapter 5: Now, let us have an exposition of YOGA

If we wish to comprehend the standards of YOGA, our brains can't be stalled before or worrying about what's to come. With every single other worry at any rate incidentally set aside, our brains are liberated to be totally at the time. The capacity to center consideration is a significant imperative in every aspect of adapting however particularly in profound issues, which contain unobtrusive philosophical perceptions.

Atha, interpreted as "now," infers Sri Patanjali's wellness or position to instruct. He is calling the class to arrange, in a manner of speaking. Just a certified instructor would do that. The word was likewise generally used to show the start of a course of study planned to evacuate questions. Concerning Raja YOGA, the uncertainty to be tended to alludes to understudies' vulnerabilities in regards to the legitimacy of the study of YOGA.

The word anusasanam, "piece," was utilized to flag the start of the investigation of a subject that either was made out of ordinarily held ideas or had been recently educated on a progressively rudimentary level. Thinking about this, it is evident that Sri Patanjali was not asserting that his was another educating yet rather that it was a clarification of what had been instructed previously. It is likewise sensible to expect that there were sure givens that Sri Patanjali didn't allude to when addressing his understudies. It resembles an educator in a theological college who realizes that it isn't important to characterize the Golden Rule or rundown the Ten Commandments when addressing his understudies.

We would now be able to reconsider this sutra and envision that Sri Patanjali's understudies may have comprehended it as, "Be alert, remain centered, for any questions you have concerning the immortal educating of YOGA will currently be eradicated."

The limitation of the alterations of the brain stuff is YOGA.

This is the core of Raja YOGA. Each word is overwhelming with importance. This sutra alone could shape a mind-blowing premise of examination and practice.

The four words that contain this sutra are, in Sanskrit: YOGAs chitta vritti nirodha.

YOGA

"YOGA" has become such a lot of a piece of our regular language that we underestimate that we comprehend its importance. Gotten from the root, yuj, it alludes to the demonstration of burdening. In like manner utilization, it alluded to the saddling of creatures to trucks so as to utilize them. It is the root from which we determine the English word "burden."

Afterward, the word was applied to the control of the faculties and alluded to tackling the intensity of a concentrated brain toward an object of love. It was then summed up to allude to any otherworldly teaches. "YOGA" is likewise used to allude to the fundamental association or Oneness of the person with the Self. This last standard, regular in the philosophical arrangement of Vedanta, has impacted the comprehension of this term in numerous schools of YOGA.

We don't need to confine our comprehension of the word to any one definition. Why exclude them all? Similarly as we esteem a gemstone for the manner in which every aspect reflects light, each importance adds broadness and profundity to our comprehension of the term. Every single profound utilization of "YOGA" can be viewed as when contemplating the word. Right now, take a gander at a fractional posting of definitions arranged from three Sanskrit word references and afterward apply them to this sutra:

YOGA: mental fixation, exertion, application, works on prompting the province of YOGA (otherworldly trains), movement, solidarity, opportunity, cure, fix, strict dynamic, undertaking, gadget, association, connection, procurement, gain, whole, wellness, attempt, enthusiasm, vehicle.

In the accompanying model, the words in enclosures allude to the definitions recorded previously. YOGA could be characterized as:

The concentrated exertion applied to the achievement of profound orders (mental fixation, exertion, application, otherworldly teaches)...

... intended to bring the expert (transport, vehicle)...

... to an end of distinguishing proof with the inner self sense, prompting the disposal of the misguided feeling of detachment from the Self (solidarity, association).

All things considered, realize that YOGA will generally be the way to expel the suffering of numbness (cure, fix)...

... and the quintessence of every single otherworldly way (strict deliberation).

Chitta

Chitta originates from the root, cit, "to see, know, watch." Translated as "brain" or "psyche stuff" all through this content, it alludes to the brain in its totality: cognizant, subliminal, and oblivious.

The chitta is certifiably not a different segment of Prakriti or a comparable to the Purusha. It is the reflected cognizance of the Purusha on Prakriti. All things considered, chitta is a method for understanding the connection between the Purusha (the Seer) and Prakriti (the seen). Since Purusha and Prakriti are ubiquitous, the chitta is additionally all-swarming, however it seems, by all accounts, to be constrained through contact with the sense of self.

The chitta is made out of three capacities: manas, buddhi, and ahamkara. In spite of the fact that these terms are not referenced in the sutra, they were usually known on account of their utilization in Sankhya theory, which imparts various standards to Sri Patanjali's YOGA.

Manas. The chronicle workforce of the chitta; that part of the psyche stuff through which impressions enter. Manas is by all accounts related with the working of the faculties. It is through manas that the individual comes into contact with outer articles.

Buddhi: two implications

It is the discriminative personnel of the brain. Buddhi takes the impressions from manas and, through a procedure of examination and separation, arranges them, permitting the impressions to be put away for access sometime in the future.

Buddhi is the primary, most perfect and most unpretentious result of the development of Prakriti. It is the contact, as it were, between Spirit (Purusha) and Nature (Prakriti). From buddhi develops ahamkara, the three gunas (constituents of Nature), the faculties, and the unobtrusive and gross components. At the point when utilized with regards to the development of Prakriti, it is additionally some of the time called mahat.

Ahamkara. Ahamkara is the self image, the feeling that we are people, separate from one another and our condition. Ahamkara claims the impressions from manas and buddhi as its own, packaging considerations together to frame the individual brain. Without ahamkara, there is no individual psyche.

The self image is something like a canine denoting its domain in a timberland. Before the pooch tagged along, the trees were basically there, having a place with nobody. At the point when the pooch adds its fragrance to the trees, it feels that they're his. The pooch currently has something to safeguard—property to stress over. Moreover, the personality stakes out the fringes of self-character and afterward applies exertion to keep up and reinforce it, while abstaining from anything it sees as undermining or disagreeable.

It is at the degree of sense of self that enduring emerges. The inner self keeps us from seeing the Purusha as our True Identity. It harbors desires and longings, gets startled, unreliable, furious, and jealous. However it is a similar inner self that encounters love, mindful, and sympathy. Things being what they are, for the sake of YOGA, what will we be approached to do with the inner self?

The yogi's first errand is to wipe out not the sense of self but rather the childishness that dirties it. At the point when this is practiced, negative attributes vanish, leaving the excellencies unblemished. Be that as it may, even a perfect self image has confinements—the sense of self, by definition, is constraint. It characterizes and keeps up our most fundamental parameter: our feeling of separateness. Illumination requires one more stage: the rising above of the inner self, a move from recognizing oneself as the body-brain to the acknowledgment of oneself as Purusha.

Vritti

Vritti: truly to spin, turn, rotate, to go on. It's a vivid term that proposes an unending and possibly confounding development. The word Sri Patanjali uses to depict the essential movement of the brain. A vritti isn't just an idea; it is the movement of shaping originations from singular contemplations that emerge in the psyche. It happens both on the cognizant and intuitive degrees of the brain. Vritti movement is the psyche's endeavor at comprehending the encounters it experiences. To an enormous degree, it decides our originations of what our identity is and the world we live in.

How about we inspect how vrittis are conceived and the manner in which they create. Suppose, for instance, that an outside improvement rouses the faculties, which brings the subsequent impression into the brain. The psyche takes that singular idea (pratyaya) and starts a tornado-like move, quickly weaving together trap of contemplations in a frantic quest for other, related musings. Through a procedure of looking at, differentiating, and ordering, singular contemplations stop their reality as secluded bits of data and become some portion of an intricate snare of thoughts.

At the present time, your brain is endeavoring to discover connections between this new data in regards to vrittis and any past encounters that appear to have an association with it. The quest for connection and examples is perpetual and programmed. At the point when we look at mists, we don't need to compel the brain to discover foxes, monsters, and manors in their arbitrary shapes; the psyche normally tries to bode well out of their swelling structures. This equivalent procedure is the means by which vritti action makes our existence—our reality, our family, our extremely self-personality. We are at the pivot of a universe that we made; we are the weavers who turn the real factors of our life. This means our experience of life is generally deflect mined by the idea of the networks we have woven. Henceforth vritti action is the act of developing and reasoning ideas of reality from mental impressions.

How does the clearly harmless demonstration of weaving musings make real factors? Isn't there a genuine, substantial universe outside of the originations that our brains build? Truly, there is a universe that exists autonomous of our view of it. Well at that point, we may ponder, shouldn't it appear to be more genuine than our psychological builds? In our every day experience, Reality, the unvarnished, unmodified truth of things, once in a while punctures our psyche's originations.

Vritti movement makes channels that can misshape discernment, specifically conceding and dismissing data. Our comprehension of the world is restricted and slanted by the inclinations and impediments that are incorporated with and result from vritti action. At the end of the day, we anticipate our concep-tion of reality onto the screen such is Life. In any case, reality peeks through our psychological develops when vritti action stops or winds down. Furthermore, when vritti movement stops, when all manners of thinking are stilled, at that point each channel is expelled from our vision, and we see Reality completely. In maybe the most giant "aha" minute an individual can have, we understand that we have been gazing into the eyes and heart of Truth from the start, nearly attacked by omniscience, inescapability, and power, however have been permitting just odds and ends of it into our brains.

The clouding intensity of spinning vrittis is just a large portion of the story; the genuine difficulty comes when we relate to the "real factors" our brain has woven. Recognizable proof with vritti action darkens our experience of our True Self. It removes us from the target truth of unadulterated experience and includes us in the show of the psyche—the move of light and shadows that is vritti action.

With the end goal for distinguishing proof to occur, a few components are required:

- Ignorance. To be ignorant or overlook that our True Identity is the Purusha.
- Egoism. The conviction that we are the body-mind.
- Vritti action. The constant conduct of the psyche to frame or discover connections. The psyche recognizes less with singular considerations, yet with examples of musings. It is the manner in which the brain reasons "reality" from mental impressions.

It is critical to accentuate that vritti action happens affected by obliviousness—overlooking our True Identity and afterward confusing the body and brain with the Self. The impacts are a lot of like being affected by liquor. You are denied of the capacity to separate, to place thoughts and encounters in the correct extent. You lose mental lucidity and judgment and endure weakened response time. Affected by liquor, improper and even odd conduct goes for typical. Affected by numbness, we can't encounter our True Identity.

Our relationship with vritti action superimposes discontinuity and confinements on the solidarity and amicability that is the Self. We lose our inward harmony and any expectation of discovering Truth or the bliss we look for. That is the reason it's anything but a misrepresentation to abridge profound life as stilling the relentless development in the psyche and the suspension of the constant recognizable proof with vrittis.

The flabbergasting orchestras of vritti action. A solitary note isn't a tune. It can't rouse or move us. Be that as it may, our consideration is excited when a note connects to a couple of other good notes, creates a cadenced heartbeat, and turns into a melodic expression. At the point when that expression joins different notes and expressions, it makes increasingly propulsive rhythms and includes the element of harmonies. Our brains become much progressively spellbound. Include contradiction and a couple of related developments to make an orchestra, and we will wind up flabbergasted. Each progression connects with us all the more profoundly in the melodic real factors the brain has developed. It is the equivalent with vritti action. The multilayered and multifaceted ideas shaped from vritti action are tempting, on the grounds that a lone idea offers little in the method for the under-standing and significance we look for.

Vritti's job in building self-character. You are at an evening gathering where you meet somebody who gets some information about your-self. Your reaction, unhesitating and regular, is that you are a bookkeeper, wedded, have three kids, and love the drama. Except if nudged, you won't relate points of interest, for example, you routinely utilize a number cruncher, kiss your girl farewell each morning, and are particularly moved by the primary demonstration of La Traviata, on the grounds that these musings (despite the fact that they add to your uniqueness) are not adequately thorough to characterize you. To put it plainly, with regards to characterizing your feeling of self, you all the more effectively and unequivocally relate to more extensive classes or comprehensive examples of thought as opposed to the individual musings themselves.

The wreckage we are in. Is dazzling that the adaptation of reality that we have made through vritti movement depends on spins of to a great extent nonsequential action in which our consideration continually moves (frequently rather uncontrollably) among a wide range of musings, convictions (both genuine and false), and recollections. You can affirm this for yourself following a couple of moments of endeavoring calm internal mindfulness.

For instance, the demonstration of arranging a gathering for your uncle's eighty-eighth birthday celebration is really a ride on an incoherent exciting ride of dispersed contemplations. As you plan the menu, you review that your uncle adores Italian nourishment. Watch as the spinning starts:

… eggplant is pleasant it's a nightshade I'm getting ravenous aren't nightshades awful for joint pain wasn't there something on the web about joint inflammation what's that sound my back damages I need another PC I can't manage the cost of one right now my sister makes incredible sauce perhaps I ought to find another line of work great, it's nearly lunch the economy isn't doing so well we need another president it's somewhat crisp in here kid, summer is practically over I sure am eager I ought to inquire as to whether she can help possibly pasta is better I can't bear the cost of a PC right now indeed, pasta is better...

This—and considerably more—occurs over the range of just a couple of seconds. Much the same as some science fiction, freak, hyperactive superspider distraught on radioactive steroids, the brain's unending spinning weaves networks of originations from discernments and recollections. Is it conceivable to for us to openly work among the numerous vritti networks—clingy with igno-rance—and not get captured?

Indeed, and Raja YOGA shows us how. Back to the insect: since not all the strands it weaves are clingy, it doesn't get trapped in its own web. Similarly, understudies of the YOGA Sutras discover that vrittis not corrupted by egotistical connection are liberated from tenacity.

How vritti movement influences recognition. How about we look at what experience resembles before vritti movement changes it. Envision yourself as a child, having squashed banana as your first strong nourishment. At that first taste, the faculties handed-off the taste, shading, surface, and fragrance to your brain. At that point, there was no sweet fruity taste, no yellow, and no banana fragrance. Your eyes shone with amazement and interest when the organic product contacted your tongue. You essentially experienced it for what it was. You were at the time, not impacted by inclinations, fears, or assumptions. At that time, you genuinely knew the idea of a banana.

Extraordinary sages and holy people everything being equal and conventions instruct that to encounter edification, we have to overlook all we have learned and become like a youngster. We have to recapture the lucidity and won-der of unadulterated experience. This honest stunningness is a piece of the enormity, the heavenliness, we see in Self-acknowledged experts. Their encounters of life, not shaded by networks of musings, are immediate, quick, and complete.

The down to earth side of vritti movement. Vritti movement gives us alternate way methods for managing the universe of encounters. A feline sees a sparrow roosted on a branch overhead. In the feline's brain, the sparrow shape falls into the class of potential supper. She intuitively prepares to jump. A similar feline, after observing the simple shadow of a bird of prey flying over-head, digs in and rushes to security. In the two cases, there is no examination required. Each feathered creature's shape fits into a classification of the feline's world: one dietary, the other a danger. It is simpler to get to data by class than by filtering through a huge number of individual, arbitrary contemplations.

At last, the issue with vritti action isn't simply the classes or connections. Rather, it is the recognizable proof with that action, established in numbness, that keeps us from considering Reality to be it genuinely is.

What Vrittis do:

•   Vrittis are the psychological exercises through which the brain stuff encounters and endeavors to comprehend and sort out the encounters of life.

•   Vrittis are framed affected by numbness.

•   When singular contemplations (pratyaya) emerge, they are stood out and looked at from different musings and afterward gathered into classifications with comparable impressions. This relentless movement can occur on a cognizant or oblivious level. The made idea networks are likewise alluded to as vrittis.

•   The movement of vrittis creates and continues a misguided feeling of personality. Like cosmologists of the Dark Ages who accepted that the earth was the focal point of the universe, vritti movement makes a fake focus of awareness, a bogus confinement for that which is inescapable. Through the procedure of distinguishing proof, vritti movement makes the dream of a self-personality separate from the Purusha.

•   Vrittis give just a constrained impression of presence and are the methods by which we anticipate our origination of reality onto items and occasions.

This carries us to nirodha, the last word in the sutra which is the exit from the negative impacts of vritti action.

Nirodha

Nirodha is utilized to signify both a procedure and a state. It is regularly interpreted as limitation, discontinuance, limitation, concealment, anticipation, control, and hindrance. The trouble with these renderings is that they now and then lead us to diminish its significance to something like "a commanding, mechanical ending of manners of thinking." And since nirodha is normally connected with rehearses for stilling the brain—making it peaceful, clear, and one-pointed—the trouble in understanding it gets aggravated. Be that as it may, nirodha's capacity to at present the action of vrittis isn't because of beast constraint, however a procedure of selec-tive center: diverting and holding consideration on one item or thought. Right now, vrittis are normally limited from awareness, breaking the standard daily schedule of vritti movement. This liberates the brain from the constant examples of observation that darken the genuine idea of life and self. The brain starts to see everything in a crisp new light, to consider things to be they are. That is the reason practices, for example, love, petition, benevolent help, and study that additionally depend on specific center lead to discharging the hold of the vrittis on the psyche.

Since it isn't simply the vrittis yet our relationship with them that causes us stress and enduring, our comprehension of nirodha ought to incorporate any procedure that closes obliviousness' hold over the brain stuff. This comprehension is reflected in Sri Patanjali's descrip-tion of flawlessness in nirodha. Note the distinction in a psyche with and without nirodha:

With nirodha

At that point the Seer (Self) resides in Its own inclination—a portrayal of Self-acknowledgment.

Without nirodha

At different occasions (the Self seems to) expect the types of the psychological changes.

Practices, fundamentals, and way of life rules are esteemed on the grounds that they encourage nirodha. Nirodha parts of the bargains goes with misidentification with the body and psyche just as obliviousness' impact over mental working.

With regards to the YOGA Sutras, nirodha is best comprehended as a multifaceted way to deal with mental authority, equipped for changing self-character. It requires the development of control, the redirection of consideration, the accomplishment of discriminative insight, the improvement of nonattachment, and is bolstered by clear good and moral standards.

Achievement of higher conditions of nirodha signals the finish of the impact of intuitive impressions (samskaras) on conduct and observation. At last, nirodha prompts the greatness of every mental confinement and the immediate acknowledgment of the person as Purusha. How does this happen?

Envision that you have never observed your own face. You've heard that it is wonderful, and now you've built up an aching to see it for yourself. However, you can't see your face since the face does the seeing. On the off chance that you need to see your face, a mirror is expected to mirror the picture back to you.

In any case, to consider yourself to be you really are, the mirror should be liberated from twisting and earth. In the event that you take a gander at your appearance in a broke, twisted, or unclean mirror, you won't consider your to be for what it's worth, you'll see a contorted picture. Seeing that you are disfigured, you become dampened. It ought to be evident that you are fine and that the twisted picture is because of a disfigured mirror, yet you continue relating to the reflected picture.

Enter Sri Patanjali. He realizes that your wretchedness is brought about by con-intertwining the reflected picture with the Self and starts delicately to manage you out of numbness. He doesn't invest a lot of energy discussing the idea of your face yet rather proposes rehearses for tenderly yet without a doubt cleaning and fixing the mirror. As you drive forward, the adjustments in the mirror cause the reflected picture to change. Gradually an awesome picture rises. At the point when the mirror turns out to be consummately straight, your face is uncovered to you as it has consistently been.

The psyche is simply the mirror where we see. On the off chance that it is mutilated by vrittis, we frequently consider ourselves to be constrained, delicate creatures, not one with the Self. We are tricked by the appearance in the psyche reflect over and over, missing reality of who we truly are. Vrittis swarm like insects, obfuscating our discriminative personnel and strengthening the broken self-appraisal that numbness intrigues on us.

Nirodha is the way to recover the memory of who we really are. We stop to relate to the vrittis. We understand that the entirety of our strife, fears, questions, outrage, and wretchedness are in the brain, not in our Self. The dramatization, struggle, humor, sentiment, experience, loathsomeness, and parody exist just fair and square of the reflection. In spite of the fact that we may revere the picture we observe, we truly haven't picked up anything we didn't as of now have; the mirror just uncovered what has consistently been. We are not the reflection but rather the face. We are the Seer, the Purusha. This is edification or Self-acknowledgment.

This is all acceptable hypothesis, yet without direct understanding of this fact, it doesn't support that much. Our brains are survivors of propensity, accustomed to eagerly running to a great extent. The brain's profoundly instilled eagerness can bring even the most powerful searchers to surrender, particularly if the main picture of nirodha they have is of sitting with folded legs, applying Herculean endeavors to keep the psyche from intuition. On the off chance that this were all there was to YOGA practice, the vast majority of us would be bound to brief professions as yogis. Luckily, this situation isn't proposed for the sake of Raja YOGA. Sri Patanjali presents an engaging, tried and true way that is clear, down to earth, and brief.

Nirodha is accomplished through a comprehensive methodology. To guarantee achievement, we are urged to use and refine all our intrinsic limits: physical, social, mental, and otherworldly. Notwithstanding stilling the psyche through fixation and reflection, we are offered numerous different methodologies that connect all of who we are in the quest for Self-acknowledgment:

- The body: YOGA stances and breath control
- The acumen: study and self-examination
- The heart: supplication and love
- Social collaboration: die hard devotion to other people
- Personal honesty: the development of good and moral ideals

By understanding the significant features and ramifications of nirodha, we can get a handle on the pith of YOGA and of every single otherworldly order.

Nirodha is practiced by redirection. The genuine mystery to gaining ground in YOGA lies in developing supportive propensities while breaking destructive ones. The best approach to grow new propensities is the intentional redirection of consideration. The roots that make up the word nirodha recommend this.

Gotten from rudh, "to limit, capture, turn away," and ni, "down or into," nirodha proposes "to deflect into." Practitioners endeavor to control their consideration from unyogic pathways by deflecting it toward attempts that are reliable with the objective of YOGA. You could think about this procedure as retraining as opposed to controlling.

Preparing the psyche resembles preparing a little dog. Having a respectful and cheerful pet is cultivated by firm, adoring redirection instead of cruel words or harsh discipline. Great pooch mentors realize this is the most ideal approach to make great propensities.

Each time we disengage our consideration from an undesirable enticement or propensity and divert it to something helpful to our development, we will have increased somewhat more dominance over our psyches.

How nirodha influences our comprehension of the world. It is hard to know an item, individual, or occasion all things considered, on the grounds that inclinations influence recognitions. It is just as we are taking a gander at life through an unsanitary camera focal point that has been inappropriately engaged.

Nirodha cleans and centers our focal point by stilling the vrittis that shading our observations. Through a perfect, centered focal point (a reasonable and consistent brain) we come to know the idea of items as they may be. The psyche normally practices its ability to infiltrate whatever is held consistent inside its core interest.

Estimating progress in nirodha. Progress in YOGA isn't neces-sarily portrayed by every day mind-twisting disclosures. Rather the way is set apart by little yet huge changes by they way we act and respond. Maybe we will be progressively quiet when cut off in rush hour gridlock. Or on the other hand we may get ourselves somewhat less dreadful or on edge when talking in broad daylight. Appreciation for fierce motion pictures might be supplanted with increasingly serene preoccupations. Next Christmas, we may choose to decrease our present spending plan with the goal that more can be given to noble cause. Sages and holy people are conceived from these beginnings.

There is one reliable indication of development: we will be increasingly tranquil and cheerful. Possibly not regularly inside and out, yet in the event that our joy were set apart on a graph, the pattern over some undefined time frame would be upward.

Nirodha, atonement and the Bible. Contrition is a significant repeating topic in the Bible. Despite the fact that we typically think about atonement as an outflow of regret, it initially intended to experience an extreme change in qualities and conduct. It implied a getting some distance from the dimness of obliviousness (corrupt ways) and toward driving an actual existence dependent on profound standards (moving in the direction of God). Both nirodha and apology speak to defining moments, key changes in goals. They structure the nexus of life for the individuals who try to end the haziness of obliviousness and the move in the direction of the Spirit.

Chapter 6: The Seer and Other Related Concepts

Seer is another method for alluding to the Purusha: unadulterated cognizance; perpetual, unconditioned mindfulness.

The word tolerate intends to abide or take changeless habitation in. In light of the psyche's steady vacillations, the Seer, however constantly present as our True Identity, appears to show up and vanish. What withstand proposes is that the Seer will never again be a guest, accompanying times of mental stillness and leaving when the psyche gets fretful.

The last two sutras present the fundamental hypothetical center of Raja YOGA; that in a flawlessly still, clear psyche, all hints of obliviousness evaporate and the individual encounters oneself as unadulterated, unceasing, unbounded mindfulness: the Self. It resembles a wave that encounters that it is presently, was, and consistently will be unified with the sea.

Eventually in your evaluation school years you were likely approached to remember a sonnet to recount the following day. What did you say on the off chance that you knew it flawlessly? "I know it by heart." Not by head, psyche, or mind, however by heart. Heart infers the totality of the psyche, something more profound and more steady than the standard reasoning contraption. To have an unadulterated heart is to have a spotless, consistent brain—a condition of nirodha. The aftereffect of this virtue is that we will see God. There is no decision suggested. On the off chance that your heart is unadulterated, you will see God; no two ways about it.

The Old Testament contains a fundamentally the same as thought. It shows up in Psalm 46.10. This time it is God speaking: "Be still and realize that I am God." Stillness is the prerequisite. Stillness; not just avoiding movement, however total stillness, similar to the quiet, away from of a lake which can reflect like a mirror.

Each one of the individuals who have accomplished nirodha have the endowment of double vision. They see the solidarity that is God behind the decent variety of names and structures. They never dismiss the Cosmic One that is the ground of all creation. How do those of us who have not achieved this grandiose state see the world? What befalls our perception of the Self when the psyche is hued by obliviousness?

At different occasions (the Self seems to) expect the types of the psychological changes.

This portrays the propensity for sticking to uniqueness: the sense of self relating to mental action. The spin of mental adjustments (vrittis) has a method for dazzling our consideration. It is a show so enrapturing that we lose ourselves (and Self) in the showy behavior. We overlook that we are truly observers to the play.

The procedure of misidentification is misleadingly honest. For instance, on the off chance that we take a gander at our bodies in a mirror, we think we are the body. "I am tall." "I am slim." "I am male." "I am wiped out."

At the point when we relate to the substance of the brain

we offer various expressions. "I am a teacher of material science." "I am a specialist." "I am cheerful." "I am pitiful."

Notice how language uncovers that our "I" seems to experience changes. However, the Self hasn't changed. It's simply the impression of the in the psyche reflect that changes. Our face, reflected in a contorted mirror, stays unaffected. Similarly, the Self stays unaffected and boundless despite the fact that it is pondered a psyche that, affected by obliviousness, is misshaped by vrittis.

There are five sorts of mental alterations, which are either excruciating or easy.

Sri Patanjali portrays vrittis in two different ways: by category and by effect.

By Category

The classes comprise of the five essential exercises that the brain performs while taking part in day by day life.

By Effect

On a very basic level, mental action is roused by a dualistic standard. The brain's consideration constantly streams in one of two directions: toward exercises that are pleasurable or away from those that bring torment. Right now, are being acquainted with a more profound comprehension.

Note the words utilized right now: "or effortless." Why not utilize the word pleasurable, the normal inverse of agonizing? We erroneously think (at times subliminally) that there is a way of thinking or set of otherworldly activities that will stop enduring and bring joy. We accept this since we overlook that the joy we look for is, in all actuality, who we as of now are. What's more, in spite of the fact that the facts confirm that vritti action has just two effects, they are not agony and delight. Truly vritti movement can either darken the satisfaction that is our actual nature or leave that bliss undisturbed.

The stream toward the easy is described by clearness, wisdom, and selflessness. This idea stream prompts the disbanding of obliviousness. Then again, mental exercises that bring torment are affected by numbness and help keep up its capacity and impact. These two major developments resemble whirlpools, picking up or losing energy as indicated by the contemplations and activities of the person.

We have gotten acclimated with the brain stream that keeps up numbness and are constantly brought into its ebbs and flows a significant part of the time. Through the acts of Raja YOGA, we increment the draw of the effortless whirlpool. Every single occurrence of reflection, petition, selfless activity, investigation of high standards, or mantra redundancy adds power to the force of easy vrittis, fortifying their impact in our lives. After some time, the agony free whirlpool increases adequate power to defeat the agonizing one. No yogic demonstration, regardless of how little, is ever squandered and adds to Self-realization.

If we look at snapshots of satisfaction and harmony, we will find that what they offer are hidden, transitory looks at the Self. They are the examples when the psyche, through a mix of elements (basically the suspension of needing), has immediately gotten steadier, empowering it to mirror a trace of the harmony inside.

Without self-propelled desires, there is nothing to upset the psyche. As my lord regularly stated, "Where there is no arrangement made, there can be no failure." The wellspring of our agony is our own arrangement or desire. The brain, when never again goaded without anyone else focused perspectives, continuously settles down, getting clear and still. Working the brain in a selfless mode doesn't directly bring joy; it just disregards the psyche so the inward euphoria can sparkle forward.

They are correct information, misperception, conceptualization, rest, and memory.

This sutra mentions to us what vrittis "resemble." If we wish to get criminals, it is useful to have a decent portrayal of what they look like or act. In the event that we will likely accomplish nirodha over the vrittis in the psyche, a portrayal of them is helpful.

These five vrittis can be assembled into three classifications. The first is worried about the manners in which we assemble data, regardless of whether legitimate or invalid. The second is something contrary to social affair information—the idea of nothing and its outcome, the state we call rest. It is the means by which the brain accomplishes a condition of profound rest. The third is memory, which makes learning conceivable by holding encounters and offering congruity to life.

Rest, recollections, and information—right or wrong—this is in the domain of mental adjustments and in this manner, as indicated by Sri Patanjali, should eventually go under our authority.

The wellsprings of right information are direct perception, inference, and authoritative testimony.

Our comprehension of life is based on an establishment of information we increase over a lifetime. In any case, that information can be believed just on the off chance that it is achieved by legitimate methods.

There are two different ways of deciphering this sutra:

• There are three dependable methods for accomplishing data with respect to life and the Self.

• A snippet of data is viewed as reliable subsequent to going through this three-pronged procedure.

Direct Perception

Data increased through direct perception can be trusted as legitimate, implying that it fits in with the established truths. By putting direct perception first, Sri Patanjali infers that experience is the foundation of the learning procedure. Experience isn't simply the best educator; it is the main instructor. Indeed, even to peruse a book or take a class is to profit by another person's understanding. We may peruse of fire that it produces warm and can be put to either ruinous or useful employments. It could all bode well, however in the event that our involvement in fire has been con-fined to words on a page, it stays a reality outside of our experience. We can't state that we know the idea of fire. However, when we put our finger close to the fire, we realize that it can consume substance; and in the wake of preparing nourishment over a fire, we will comprehend its advantage. Accepting that our faculties are working regularly, direct perception is a wellspring of information that we can trust and use in our examination of the world and our deepest Self.

Direct perception is the underlying effect of an improvement on singular cognizance. Notwithstanding, when the psychological capacities kick in, what was an unadulterated direct encounter can get shaded by the constraints of the manner of thinking itself. In the event that there is an absence of center during the demonstration of perception, the information picked up can be fragmented. At that point, when the self image, ahamkara, stamps its engraving on that understanding, asserting it as exceptional to itself, the experience generally gets shaded by inclinations, wants, repugnances, and fears. At long last, while reviewing the experience, the psyche gets helpless against the tainting impacts of broken or fragmented memory, making imperative realities be lost or unessential data included.

Since we can't directly encounter everything ourselves, we should have the option to pick up information from different sources. For instance, we routinely gather and procedure data through perusing or tuning in. (On the off chance that the wellspring of the data is viewed as master, we would then utilize authoritative testimony, the third category for achieving right information.) The information we accumulate structures an interior library of data: genuine, bogus, or blended. This put away data, when used to enlarge direct perception, is what is known as inference.

Inference

Inference, basically a component of the discriminative staff of the brain (buddhi), depends on recently picked up information. It necessitates that we know probably a portion of the qualities of the article being derived and can accurately relate those attributes to the item. The exemplary model is that fire can be derived when we see smoke, since it is realized that one trait of fire is that it is joined by smoke.

Inference as a method for achieving information is just as dependable as the explanatory methods utilized. In the event that I spot smoke ascending on a removed peak, I can surmise the nearness of fire, however simply after I deflect mine whether what I see is genuinely smoke, not a wispy cloud, steam getting away from a plant vent, or residue kicked up by a truck. Essentially observing a dim, rolling shape noticeable all around doesn't give enough data to draw a substantial inference. In any case, I might have the option to accurately gather fire on the off chance that I move nearer and distinguish the smell of smoke or hear the sound of a fire engine drawing closer. Any endeavor to decisively recognize what I'm seeing before get-together adequate data would hop an end.

The brain's propensity to make a hasty judgment is presumably one motivation behind why Sri Patanjali might want us to think about the best possible approach to make inferences. Consider how much difficulty is caused when the brain expects realities not in proof. Misleading allegations and relational hardship are just piece of the issue. Our brains can get covered with deceptions and misleading statements about existence and the world we live in. So as to maintain a strategic distance from this risky propensity, it is useful to know about the perspective that makes it almost certain.

The essential factor that imprints forming a hasty opinion is an interference or defilement of the reality gathering process due to:

- Loss of focus in the demonstration of perception

- The anxiety to encounter something we think will bring us delight

- The nervousness to evade what we think will bring us torment Ideally, in what capacity should the procedure of inference work?

The Sanskrit expression for inference, anumana, holds significant pieces of information for the effective examination of data. It originates from the roots, anu, "after," and mama, "to show, measure, get ready." "To show after" can be comprehended as the utilization of memory; "to quantify" recommends appraisal; and "to plan" suggests the making of a determination. Thusly, inference is the way toward making a sensible determination with respect to an encounter through precise review and appraisal.

Exact memory. In contrast to direct perception, in which the article itself is the improvement for (and the focal point of) perception, in inference, it is a quality of the item that grabs our eye.

Model: I put a sweet potato dish in the stove. In the interim, I occupied myself with some extraordinary housecleaning. After two hours, I get a whiff of something disturbing. My memory, scanning for comparative scents, rapidly reports that the fragrance I am recognizing is that of consuming nourishment. I have not directly watched the consuming nourishment yet have seen one of its attributes. The undesirable fragrance at that point blends another memory: I review the dish that I put in the broiler two hours sooner.

For inference to be of significant worth, memory should be precise and promptly available. Exact memory is upgraded by having a reasonable, centered psyche unrestricted by predisposition or individual connection.

Evaluation. Since inference manages qualities, I should have the option to discover connections between the trademark I am encountering and its item. In the event that my comprehension of the connection delivers between what I am encountering and that which is being induced is right, and if my psyche follows a coherent movement of reason and opposes forming a hasty opinion out of tension, dread, or some other stressor, my proportion of the occasion is something I can depend on as precise.

Model: Using the data I have within reach, I evaluate that my memories of the smell of consumed nourishment and an overcooked meal have a consistent relationship.

Reaching an inference. This is the way toward abridging data into usable information.

Model: I infer that it is my sweet potato meal that is consuming. Direct visual perception of my goulash will check my inference.

Drawing a sensible and obvious end result about a thought, item, or occasion permits us to discover correspondences to different snippets of data and may likewise incite us to shape general standards or strategies. In the above model, I rapidly choose to expel the meal from the broiler and afterward search for a stove clock with an uproarious chime.

Authoritative Testimony

Agama, actually, "to go toward a source," is master counsel and direction from sacred writings and from profound adepts or illuminated people.

The direct understanding of sages, holy people, prophets, and profound bosses is a substantial wellspring of information, since it is information that has demonstrated its unwavering quality to incalculable searchers after some time. It ought to likewise be information that can possibly be checked by the person through their own direct perception. We can confirm the legitimacy of our manual's guides when we drive the streets for ourselves.

Presently we should analyze how direct perception, inference, and authoritative testimony cooperate to help guarantee that any information picked up is exact and hence valuable in thinking about profound lessons.

Expecting that the faculties are in acceptable working request, there is no dream in direct perception. In this manner, it is a legitimate wellspring of social occasion information. However, it has commonsense confinements. The extent of learning is constrained to individual encounters. Additionally, there are no ideas, words, esteem decisions—no chance to get of imparting the experience to other people or of evaluating its motivation throughout everyday life. In spite of the fact that the data is valid, it is distinct and separated from different realities.

Inference permits us to work with data. We think about, differentiate, and assess bits of data on numerous levels, refining them until they can be utilized in regular day to day existence. Inference not just carries our encounters into the world yet helps us in planning, sorting out, and using all the information we obtain. Be that as it may, as we noted over, the procedure of inference is helpless to the twisting impact of the manners of thinking. This is the place authoritative testimony comes in.

So as to demonstrate that individual information is sound, it is judicious to gauge it against master, target testimony.

How about we take a gander at a speculative guide to show how the three wellsprings of right information balance one another. Assume that you have repeating episodes of stomach inconvenience. The impression of torment is direct understanding. Your anxiety spurs you to allude to a few clinical writings, examine on the Internet, and converse with a couple of companions who have had comparable issues. Through inference you reason that it is an instance of heartburn. You infer that it isn't not kidding and buy over-the-counter medications to treat it.

Obviously, you could possibly be right. In the event that you wish to be sure, or if the endeavors at self-medication demonstrate fruitless, you would normally counsel specialists—specialists. So also, in the event that we wish to affirm the legitimacy of our comprehension of profound issues, we would do well to counsel authoritative writings and the individuals who have encountered the realities of these lessons for themselves.

This three-limbed way to deal with increasing seeing—direct perception, inference, and authoritative testimony—helps keep the yogi's consideration centered around tries that are helpful for their otherworldly development.

Misperception happens when information on something did not depend on its actual structure.

The word interpreted as misperception is viparyaya. The word's underlying foundations offer a piece of information into what it is and how it happens.

Viparyaya is from I, "to go, stream," with vi, "in two, away," and pari, "around," offering Viparyaya, "to stream away or around."

Misperception happens when the brain overlooks what's really important and streams from or around reality when making inference about an event.

Note how this meaning of misperception is nearly the direct inverse of nirodha—holding the psyche's consideration consistent. The suggestion is that perceptions can be defective when the psyche needs consistent core interest. Misperception is grounded in issues that happen during the demonstration of perception or during the time spent inference. It may be the case that the data transferred by the faculties is deficient, the rationale is flawed, insignificant data is included, or the memory doesn't contain realities relevant to the article apparent. The result of misperception is that psychological impressions (vrittis) that don't compare to undeniable realities become put away and treated as evident information.

The exemplary case of misperception is confusing a wound rope with a snake in a faintly lit room. The mixed up perception delivers a similar effect as though the snake were really present.

Misperceptions for the most part contain a bit of truth. Proceeding with our model, the faculties effectively saw a looped shape and handed-off that data to the discriminative workforce. Perhaps due to a profound dread of snakes or in light of the fact that the memory of a narrative on poisonous snakes was new in our brain, the organized procedure of inference was shortcircuited. We bounced to an end that didn't compare to the real world. Without mental serenity, we are handily diverted demonstrations of perception or inference. Our brains, tossed into an uncontrolled chain response of intuitive impressions, wants, and inclinations, falls prey to misperception.

It is fascinating to take note of that Sankhya theory records the reasons for misperception as:

- Egoism
- Aversion
- Ignorance
- Clinging to substantial life/self-love
- Attachment

Information that depends on language alone, autonomous of any outside item, is conceptualization.

The psyche builds our comprehension of life through different roads. Information conceived of conceptualization depends on language alone: on our nature with words and the information symbolized by words. Conceptualization is the making of abstract real factors from the psyche's unending inward discoursed. It is maybe the most productive maker of our thoughts of the real world. Consider for a minute what number of our thoughts concerning presence are shaped from or depend on what we hear in discussions and through books, papers, films, TV shows, and verses.

In conceptualization, the psyche weaves real factors by joining memory and language in different innovative manners. Note that information increased through conceptualization could possibly be right. For instance, think about the maxim, "Love is visually impaired," a recommendation with no recognizable article that we can interface with it. It is a reality developed of words alone that may to be sure mirror a reality. Next, we experience the idiom, "God is love." once more, there is no article discernible by the faculties, and again—utilizing just words—we treat these words as a reality. These two maxims reverberation, in a beautiful way, individual emotions that are genuine and that can become building squares of our perspective. In any case, until we experience the items related with these conceptualizations (love in one case, and God in the other) or have them affirmed by authoritative testimony, we can't regard these platitudes as right information. Here's one valid justification: conceptualization can undoubtedly turn crazy and lead us into obliviousness. Utilizing a sort of condition based manner of thinking, we can show up at another "truth" by consolidating the two adages above: If love is visually impaired and God is love, in this manner God is visually impaired. With no outside article to control our brains from dream or no recognized authority adjusting us, we may enjoy flights of extravagant. These psychological journeys can take us from word-recipes that mirror a fact to awesome pictures gathered from recollections: a thirty-foot crab with a pony's head, for instance. The way that conceptualization can make us surrender appropriate inference, authoritative direction, and direct perception for word-developed truths is pleasantly portrayed in the

Sanskrit for conceptualization, vikalpa. Its root makes an interpretation of as "to withdraw from the very much arranged or appropriate."

Since conceptualizations have no outside perspective, they can cloud our perception of reality as it genuinely seems to be. We can contemplate demanding analogies portraying the flavor of a banana, however until we really taste one, it stays a conceptualization—a reality not experienced. For yogic understudies who are keen on direct perceptions of the real world, the profoundly imbued propensity for conceptualization:

- Forms squares to direct perception
- Distracts the psyche from the rationale of inference
- Hinders us from profiting by the astuteness that originates from authoritative testimony

Information increased through conceptualization isn't viewed as substantial until and except if there is a real article or occasion that is directly seen or in the event that it very well may be certified by an authoritative source. Every single certifiable truth can be confirmed, so, all in all they are then viewed as authoritative testimony: a "wellspring of right information".

Conceptualization has a positive side. It is the means by which we structure the allegories and comparisons that assist us with understanding information put away in the psyche. Conceptualization likewise frames the premise of the imaginative procedure important to create verse and different expressions.

Comparison between Misperception and Conceptualization

As opposed to misperception, in which the psyche changes the perception of an outer article, conceptualization is without any item, any comparing reality. In misperception, we confused a rope with a snake. Here there is only the intensity of language to make vrittis.

One of the manners in which we fall into the traps of conceptualization is the point at which the quest for truth is relinquished for things dreaded or sought after. In such cases, depending on conceptualization as a wellspring of legitimate information regularly prods the psyche to make a hasty judgment.

There is an anecdotal story of a small schoolboy, about 15 years old, who was starting out as an athlete in high jump. He was describing to his schoolmates—and any other individual who might tune in—the astounding occasions that happened at the area titles.

He gladly told his companions that on his first high jump attempt, he tied the school record. The group cheered uncontrollably. Yet, tragically, he accentuated, he was unable to demonstrate this happened in light of the fact that nobody was there to see it. His schoolmates were stunned at his achievement.

His next high jump broke the state record. The group bounced to its feet, cheering in loud recognition.

"I realize this is difficult to accept, however it's valid. The main sadness I have is that nobody was there who can check or verify my story."

"Stunning!" shouted one of his companions. "What a disgrace that the media was not there."

On his last high jump attempt, the group became quieted as the bar was raised over the national record. He summoned his fixation, concentrated on the crossbar, and, in a relentless exertion, broke the record. The group, again on its feet, cheered long and hard, reciting expressions of recognition for their old neighborhood legend. "In any case, unfortunately," the youngster stated, "nobody was there to see it."

At that point one little youngster stated, "Nobody was there to see this?" "No," answered our legend, "nobody."

Another cohort ringed in, "However the group... the group applauded you, didn't they?" "Why, yes they did."

Out of nowhere, they comprehended. With boisterous murmurs and moving eyes, they started to leave. Gotten up to speed in the dramatization of his story, they had fallen casualties to him using conceptualization on them.

In our everyday lives, when we take in realities or occasions from words alone, it is helpful to permit the psyche time to analyze the related conditions and, when pertinent, counsel "specialists." Often, we can maintain a strategic distance from the issues that follow from forming a hasty opinion.

That psychological alteration which relies upon the idea of nothingness is rest.

This alludes to dreamless rest. It is the state wherein all different vrittis are suspended, then again, actually of nothingness. The way that we dozed demonstrates that rest isn't the unimportant nonattendance of mental movement. We recall just that which we see.

Albeit profound rest furnishes the body with much-required recuperating rest, the more profound and increasingly unobtrusive capacity of rest is the revival of the brain. The body, however it needs rest so it can recover, can get some recovery in different ways. For the propelled yogi, profound conditions of contemplation give significant rest and revival to both the body and psyche.

Memory is the memory of experienced items

All encounters sway the psyche as vrittis. After a period, the vrittis become subtler and sink to the base of the psychological lake, where they become samskaras: subliminal impressions. Samskaras can lie lethargic and not influence us, become dynamic on an intuitive level and impact our cognizant mental states, or get animated and come back to the outside of the psychological lake as a memory.

This sutra has a connect to the past one. Dreams are recollections that stand up for themselves in rest. These recollections may introduce them-selves in emblematic structure as are frequently not perceived thusly.

Memory is the just one of the five idea waves that worries the past. Without it, we were unable to gain for a fact.

These psychological alterations are limited by training and nonattachment.

This two dimensional methodology encapsulates a guideline utilized by all encompassing social insurance professionals. While fitting treatment for the present grumbling is endorsed, measures that fortify protection from future events are additionally recommended. Practice is undifferentiated from treatment, and nonattachment, to counteraction. Both practice and nonattachment are important for achievement in YOGA. They are integral methodologies that help the psyche become more clear, more settled, and more grounded.

Practice without nonattachment can prompt a superinflated personality that relishes utilizing capacity to fulfill self-intrigue paying little mind to outcomes. Numerous evil presences in Hindu folklore were propelled yogis who tumbled from the way of exemplary nature when they capitulated to a terrible imperfection, normally a consuming desiring. Then again, without the quality and mental lucidity picked up from training, genuine nonattachment may never truly day break. Rather, the brain can slip into lack of concern. This fake nonattachment can give an impermanent sanctuary to the frightful—an otherworldly veneer where they can cover up so as to keep away from difficulties and obligations. At the point when fears stay immaculate, intrinsic limits stay unfamiliar. We become Clark Kent, never realizing that Superman exists in. It is practice that mines our undiscovered internal assets.

The blend of training and nonattachment prompts turning into a person who builds up their abilities without limit and who is guided by a reasonable, selfless brain.

Of these two, exertion toward consistent quality is practice.

"Exertion toward consistent quality" alludes to centering and stilling the brain in contemplation, to the development of normality, and to building up a steady consciousness of the psyche's exercises (particularly the inner self's restricting and hurtful effect). In the most broad sense, practice is the proceeded with exertion to remain inside the stream (the propensity for) mental action that prompts the disintegration of numbness.

The practices introduced in the YOGA Sutras fall into the accompanying classes:

- The physical acts of asana and pranayama
- Meditation (dharana, dhyana, samadhi)
- Devotion to God or self-give up (Ishwara Pranidhana)
- Understanding and tolerating languishing as an assistance over cleaning (tapas)
- Discriminative insight (viveka)
- Study (svadhyaya)

In every one of these practices, great outcomes can be gotten just when the psyche achieves consistent mindfulness to the job needing to be done.

Be that as it may, YOGA practice isn't constrained to formal contemplation or petition. Day by day life is the phase whereupon vrittis play out their move. Thusly our lives—each demonstration—ought to mirror an unmistakable and consistent focal point of psyche. We won't gain agreeable ground in the event that we practice control of the brain for an hour daily and afterward let it eagerly meander during the other twenty-three. Our way of life and condition should bolster our objectives. That is the reason we have to live completely at the time and to create mindful spotlight on whatever errand is close by. That is likewise YOGA practice.

By utilizing "exertion," this sutra advises us that YOGA isn't for the languid. Nothing incredible was ever accomplished without exertion. Take, for instance, the incredible artist Fred Astaire. We see him nimbly floating and jumping—apparently insusceptible to the law of gravity—and are stunned. How easy his developments appear. However numerous individuals don't have the foggiest idea how hard he attempted to accomplish that dominance. Commonly, the cast and group would return home in the wake of a difficult day's shooting just to restore the following morning to find that he had never left the studio. He kept practicing as the night progressed, endeavoring to consummate each unobtrusive subtlety of the move. His story isn't one of a kind. It is shared by numerous ladies and men who accomplished enormity.

It is huge that this sutra doesn't make any reference to partisan customs. Sri Patanjali doesn't make reference to anything explicit to Hinduism, Buddhism, Islam, or some other religion. He doesn't specify God, Truth, or Cosmic Consciousness. At the point when it comes time to characterize practice, Sri Patanjali exhibits the comprehensiveness of his comprehension by basically introducing consistent quality of psyche as the establishment of profound practice.

That is the reason it's anything but a stretch to state that when a Catholic implores the rosary, it is basically what the YOGA Sutras characterize as YOGA practice. It is the equivalent with a Buddhist priest occupied with strolling contemplation in the wildernesses of Thailand and the Jew who respectfully implores before the Western Wall in Jerusalem or the Muslim confronting Mecca in supplication. They might know the name "YOGA," however as indicated by the expert regarding the matter, they are occupied with YOGA practice.

Experience It

In the event that you haven't done so as of now, presently is a decent time to start an everyday schedule of YOGA. It's a smart thought to incorporate practices that help make the body more grounded and increasingly loose, reflection or potentially petition to help consistent the psyche, and in any event a little report to help keep roused and on target.

Think about beginning a profound journal. Make an every day outline posting all the practices you expect to perform, and note to what extent you go through with each training. You can likewise keep tabs on your development in different territories that need improvement, for example, dietary changes, ideals to develop, and negative propensities to dispose of. You could likewise devise an arrangement of fortifications to support you if and when you slip from your duties. You could include an additional sitting of contemplation or do a couple of additional rounds of breathing practices, for instance.

Note how slips by in your duties influence the nature of your practices and the manner in which you experience your day. A late night today may make tomorrow's contemplation dull and unfocused. Missing reflection by and large may get an expansion crabbiness during the day.

Audit your purposes each month or somewhere in the vicinity and update them as you progress.

A profound journal can fill in as a decent token of your destinations.

Be functional in organizing your program. Gauge how much time you need for your different obligations and practically ascertain how a lot of time you can go through with your YOGA rehearses. Understudies are frequently eager in the first place and take on more than they can realistically handle. It is smarter to invest less energy and be ordinary than a lot of time every so often.

Try not to be fixated on your advancement. Indeed, even an outing to a get-away goal can appear to be wearisome when we as a whole we care about is showing up. The tension will make us miss numerous lovely and advantageous sights en route. Figure out how to acknowledge and appreciate the procedure.

Practice turns out to be immovably grounded when all around took care of for quite a while, without break, and with energy.

What is an "immovably grounded" practice and for what reason is it an alluring state? A solidly grounded practice is one that happens every day without strain or hesitant support. It is significant, motivated, and centered. It is an euphoric propensity that goes with experts for the duration of their lives and turns into the solid string that guides them to Self-realization.

A solidly grounded practice isn't just an instilled daily practice of profound activities however a foreseen time of association with more profound degrees of self. It is a period of developing associate with our True Identity, of profound disclosure and nurturance. Times by and by are seasons of joining and expanding completeness. This vision of training is the perfect and is feasible by any individual who follows the counsel introduced right now.

The achievement of a solidly grounded practice denotes a significant stage in otherworldly interests: it is the move from "doing YOGA" to having YOGA practice become a characteristic articulation of what our identity is. Practices are never again exercises outside us— methods or observances that have been added to our day by day life. Practices become as essential to our background as eating and dozing.

However, most professionals realize that there are times when practice is definitely not a lovely encounter. Introductory eagerness—the expectation and energy to encounter the harmony and delight of higher otherworldly states—can step by step offer approach to smugness and heedlessness. These are times when quite a bit of our vitality is spent on wheedling, convincing, and once in a while in any event, threatening ourselves to rehearse. At the point when practice is unpredictable, the sought after advantages are not understood, prompting a descending winding of even less incessant, less engaged practice. To keep away from this entanglement, Sri Patanjali offers a basic, effective equation for developing an immovably grounded practice.

Long Time

Achievement in any beneficial undertaking requires time, and with respect to accomplishing nirodha, quite a while. How much time relies upon factors, for example, past exercises, personality, and current condition. Be that as it may, boss among these is how a lot of exertion and center we put into our practices.

We are not advised to what extent we should trust that our practices will be immovably grounded, however unmistakably we have to have a proportion of tolerance. What can be said is that achievement in profound undertakings requires determination.

Without Break

Any understudy would love her or his training to be as

instilled a propensity as toothbrushing. In the event that you conclude today to skip tomorrow first thing's dental daily practice, there is a decent possibility that tomorrow you will end up before the restroom reflect with a mouth loaded with froth, having totally overlooked the earlier day's determination. Such is the intensity of propensity. YOGA practice can likewise turn into that routine.

To accomplish a simple, streaming consistency by and by, an extensive timeframe isn't sufficient. The training must be ordinary. There is no absence of YOGA professionals who whine that they are very little happier now than ten years back when they started. On the off chance that you question them, you will frequently find that however they have been rehearsing for a long time, their training has been a here and there issue. Progress can't be made without consistency—in YOGA as well as in any advantageous undertaking.

Notwithstanding, no exertion in YOGA is squandered. Each mantra rehashed, each asana, each event of die-hard devotion to other people, each petition, demonstration of love, or bit of holy information learned adds to the force and profundity of training.

With Enthusiasm

Long stretches of ordinary practice despite everything probably won't produce the normal outcomes in the event that it isn't finished with the correct disposition. Excitement intends to have confidence and love for the practices and what they will bring. The key empowers us to rehearse for quite a while and without break.

Before all else, excitement is enlivened by the guarantee of advantages to come. As we progress, the harmony and delight of the Self unfolding on the psyche turns into the extraordinary helper.

YOGA is a science. On the off chance that you practice tirelessly, you'll get the outcomes. There is no uncertainty about it. We form into better individuals, looking for inside ourselves to discover where commitment lives, where consistency is the characteristic state, and where the underlying foundations of love are covered up. We could supplant, "long time, without break, and in all genuineness" with "commitment, consistency, and love." These characteristics will work well for us in any undertaking.

How might we tell if our training has gotten solidly grounded? One straightforward answer is: the point at which it is more diligently not to rehearse than to rehearse. Another touchstone is: when, for reasons outside your ability to control, rehearses are missed. Does skirting a day or two or a difference in plan start a course of abnormality? Assuming this is the case, the training isn't yet immovably grounded. The individuals who have solidly settled their training are not lost by changes in timetable, spot, or time. For them, the delight and advantages of the practices are more grounded than common interruptions.

Committed practice creates a progression of mental vitality toward Self-realization so solid and indispensable that no other outcome can follow. In the event that we continue advancing that stream, we will some time or another experience help (grace) as the draw of the Absolute.

Chapter 7: Nonattachment

Nonattachment is simply the indication authority in one who is liberated from longing for objects seen or caught wind of.

Nonattachment, vairagya, truly signifies "without shading." It is the capacity to keep the bends of selfish thought processes and purposes out of each relationship, activity, and procedure of learning.

Selfish wants are the average persuading powers of the psyche, pulling it toward sought after delight or away from the fear of torment. In any case, for those keen on Self-realization, selfish wants are not the proper method of working, since they depend on alleviating the uneasiness of needing and not on what is genuinely, intellectually, socially, or profoundly valuable. Searchers are approached to develop an alternate establishment for their activities: nonattachment.

Nonattachment develops when the psyche deliberately changes its basic inspirations from selfish to selfless, from looking for sense fulfillment to looking for an encounter of harmony that rises above outside conditions. Selfless wants bit by bit discharge the psyche from the influence of sense-spurred action and open it to the incredible impact of the Purusha.

Relating nonattachment to self-authority may lead us to con-intertwine it with over the top activities in suppression and self-hardship. That way regularly prompts disappointment and an unequal perspective on the world as a perilous and fiendishness place. Rather, the self-dominance that communicates as nonattachment is a procedure of re-teaching the psyche through:

- The cautious perception of the restrictions of sense fulfillment; it is the development of reasonable, sound associations with articles and achievements dependent on understanding what the world can and can't offer.
- The exertion to live as indicated by rules that encourage otherworldly development as opposed to what feels great right now
- Cultivating an inward mindfulness: a reflective mentality that knows about the intentions in activities
- The redirection of the will when settling on decisions; not by constraint of wants however by directing the consideration away from selfish activities and toward those that are selfless

Yet, these clarifications are most likely insufficient to motivate certain, eager practice. It is difficult to drop the inclination that nonattachment is by one way or another unnatural; that it rejects human feelings and advances a bleak perspective on life. That is the reason achievement in nonattachment requires a more profound comprehension of the idea of connections and of why we are being approached to keep away from them.

Connections are attractions we feel toward items or individuals that we accept have brought us delight. Revultion, the sentiment of shock for specific items or occasions that we think bring uneasiness, is connection in turn around.

As searchers, we now and again wind up trapped in a logical inconsistency. We accept that it is nonsensical to anticipate that the world should give changeless satisfaction. In the mean time, even as we endeavor to encounter the unbounded Peace that is our True Identity, we stick to a rundown of things we think we should be cheerful. This logical inconsistency happens in light of the fact that we constantly credit the ability to present joy onto items and accomplishments.

We get a whiff of warm crusty fruit-filled treat. Promptly, with no obvious idea, a hankering creates. Longing for, never an agreeable state, pushes us vigorously. We use the time, vitality, and assets important to get some pleasant crusty fruit-filled treat. In the wake of appreciating a cut, an idea emerges. It might appear to be innocuous, yet it epitomizes a perspective that prompts enduring: "That fulfilled me." Our convictions appeared to have changed from "Bliss is my True Nature," to "I can't be cheerful without crusty fruit-filled treat." What occurred?

We used exertion to get the pie, driven by the uneasiness of the hankering and the expectation of encountering delight from fulfilling that hankering. In the wake of eating the pie, we felt a discharge and, confusing it with bliss, credited our joy to the pie. In reality, we just came back to the state we were in before the hankering grabbed hold of the psyche, though with more calories and sugar in our circulation system.

It is not necessarily the case that crusty fruit-filled treat is terrible—or acceptable. It is nonpartisan. Things in Nature are nonpartisan. It is our methodology that decides if sense objects are experienced as wellsprings of agony or delight. To keep up a reasonable, adjusted psyche; to see things as they may be, without inclination; and to act without prejudging, establish the center of nonattachment.

Your own involvement in fleeting sense delights will disclose to you that they are frequently blended with blame or the agony of seeing them gradually disappear. Once in a while, if at any point, are we impeccably fulfilled. Frequently we are left needing somewhat more or better nourishment, films, shoes, cash, or connections. This absence of genuine fulfillment is inalienable in the mixed up thought that something outside us can satisfy us. The more we depend outwardly world for satisfaction, the more we experience disappointment and needing. We overlook that an undisturbed perspective mirrors the embodiment of our being, the Self, which is satisfaction itself. The oddity is that the main path not to encounter flawless joy is to look for it outside the Self.

One may ponder: Does the act of nonattachment require avoiding things we love, those things that bring delight? Isn't it regular, even great, to need a significant activity or a caring accomplice; would they say they aren't, in any event, special cases to this standard? Didn't God make the universe for us to appreciate?

Nonattachment isn't a refutation of the world however the development of the proper relationship to the short lived delights and agonies of the world. It isn't sense protests that cause misery yet our unseemly relationship to them dependent on unreasonable, frequently selfish, desires.

Chapter 8: Samadhis of the YOGA Sutras

Cognitive (samprajnata) samadhi (is associated with structures and) is gone to by examination, insight, joy, and pure I-am-ness.

In YOGA, higher conditions of awareness are for the most part alluded to by the term samadhi, a word generally deciphered as contemplation, super-conscious state, or absorption. Before going on to the editorial for this sutra, how about we take a brief overview of the condition of samadhi, since it is fundamental to understanding YOGA philosophy and practice.

In a general sense, samadhi is a method for attaining information that is supra (above)- rational. Samadhi differs radically from our standard technique for gaining understanding in that there are no means of logic and no comparing or contrasting of bits of information in request to arrive at an understanding of the article being pondered. Instead, information gained from samadhi is direct, unconstrained, and intuitive, the result of achieving probably some significant proportion of unity with the article being thought about.

Despite the fact that the insights uncovered in samadhi are not the result of a rational point of view, they don't contradict rationality, however rise above it. Samadhi (and YOGA hypothesis and practice by and large) is not an excursion into an irrational mental scene where flights of extravagant principle the day. Review that Sri Patanjali designated inference as one of three valid methods for attaining "right information". In any case, since samadhi has the ability to go past the confines of the physical faculties, individual biases, and the inherent limitations of relativistic manners of thinking, it finishes and verifies information gained through direct perception, inference, and authoritative testimony.

Samadhi is an excursion of exploration that begins by learning to hold consistent attention on an "impact," a perceivable part of Prakriti—for practical purposes, whatever the practitioner has picked as the article for meditation. The mind at that point normally tests that object in request to discover its immediate reason, for example, a progressively unobtrusive component. The discovery of the immediate reason doesn't end the excursion, since it also was brought into being by other, much progressively unobtrusive components. The excursion continues as layer after layer of issue is stripped away until we arrive at the mother everything being equal: pure undifferentiated Prakriti.

In any case, another fundamental part of samadhi ought to be comprehended if we are to comprehend its various categories discussed in the YOGA Sutras: we have to comprehend what befalls the mind in conditions of samadhi. Here as well, samadhi is a procedure of evolution in turn around in which the components that shaped our individual mind—our very sense and experience of self—are uncovered. This journey to Self-discovery happens as we follow back the demonstration of perception to its generally unobtrusive and fundamental root, the conscience sense. We at that point rise above even that to experience our True

Identity as the pure, unceasing, unbounded consciousness that yogis call Purusha.

Keeping in mind what we have discussed up to this point regarding samadhi, we can comprehend that the levels or categories of samadhi that are found in the YOGA Sutras are essentially founded on two elements:

- The relative nuance of issue the mind is perceiving
- The degree to which the individual mind (manas, buddhi, ahamkara) and subconscious impressions continue to be active during the time spent perception

Presently we are prepared to consider the samadhis of this sutra.

The first classification of samadhi introduced in the YOGA Sutras is alluded to as cognitive (acquiring information or understanding) since it is set apart by the attainment of information regarding the object of contemplation. It is a suprarational method of functioning that brings insights regarding parts of Creation.

In samprajnata samadhi, the mind centers around some part of Creation in request to reveal its inner realities, the causes behind the impacts. It identifies with (by becoming united with) the object of contemplation. Familiar, everyday points of view are supplanted by another method for perceiving and gaining information. Instead of the acquisition of information that is categorized, analyzed, and appeared differently in relation to different bits of information (fundamental vritti activity), information gained in samprajnata samadhi is unconstrained and intuitive.

The samprajnata samadhis listed in this sutra compare to the four phases of Prakriti's evolution: net issue, unpretentious components, sattwa (pure mind), and the personality sense.

- Gross components (bhutas)

Individual items or parts of creation perceivable by the sense organs. Net components include material items perceivable by the faculties. Samprajnata samadhi at this level is said to be gone to by "examination."

- Subtle components (tanmatras)

Sound, contact, sight, taste, and smell. They are the reason for the gross components. At this degree of samprajnata samadhi, the mind gains intuitive information on the unobtrusive idea of the object of meditation and is said to be gone to by "insight."

- The mind (made out of pure sattwa)

Samprajnata samadhi at this level is gone to by "joy," the experience of the still, pure, sattwic mind.

- Pure Ego-Sense (asmita)

Feeling of individuality; the immediate reason for the mind.

Samprajnata samadhi at this level is gone to by "pure I-am-ness." fundamentally, the four phases of samprajnata samadhi describe a mind that is probing the wonder of perception, of what constitutes experience.

Our daily experiences are comprised of two factors that change and one that doesn't. The article and action change, however the subject consistently remains the same. I toss the ball. I eat the raisins. I enjoy nightfalls. I rest in the visitor room. The "I" can toss, eat, enjoy, or rest. "I" can do substantially more: skip, read, build, sniffle, or drive, for instance. The objects of these actions can be practically limitless, as well. Be that as it may, the self image, the feeling of "I," remains the same. So, samprajnata samadhi can likewise be comprehended as a procedure in which the demonstration of perception is progressively decreased to its most natural viewpoint: self image sense.

We should examine each degree of samprajnata samadhi in more detail.

Examination

Vitarka, the word deciphered as examination, can likewise be interpreted as discussion, reasoning, or question. It accompanies samadhi, in which the emphasis is on items or components that are tangible to the faculties.

Learning is a characteristic impulse. It is the idea of the engaged mind to continually test all the more profoundly into the object of attention. It needs to know more, to discover and investigate.

In vitarka samadhi, the procedure of examination is controlled by a mind that has achieved a proportion of union with the item being pondered. It is examination in its freest, most creative expression. The engaged mind normally reveals increasingly more profound and subtler degrees of the object of attention. It pierces through layers of gross issue, revealing the item's inner structure, the tanmatras or unpretentious components.

The information gained through vitarka samadhi stops at the degree of the tanmatras. In request to see the unpretentious components, the mind should be significantly progressively engaged. This brings us to vichara.

Insight

Vichara, insight, can likewise be deciphered as reflection, inquiry, introspection, or investigation. It is a more refined type of inquiry than vitarka and is performed on the tanmatras.

Like vitarka, there is no asking of questions. It is a matter of the mind attuning itself to the degree of the inconspicuous components. Information—intuitive insight—comes through attaining reverberation or identification with the object of contemplation.

Imagine what it might be want to meditate on taste. Not the flavor of something, yet simply taste or sight, hearing or contact. What about development, time, or space? These are difficult to imagine without tangible articles to relate them to. However, in the vichara samadhis, this is finished. These unpretentious items might be specifically picked by the practitioner or can come as a characteristic result of the vitarka samadhis.

Joy

'Ananda' is the Sanskrit word for bliss or joy. This samadhi is the experience of the pure (sattwic) part of the mind which is past the unpretentious components. It is the bliss of a mind liberated from worries, stress, fears, and weights. The joy of ananda samadhi is infinitely more satisfying than our standard experiences of happiness, since the mind mirrors the unbounded joy that is the Self.

As awesome as the experience of ananda samadhi may be, we shouldn't mistake it for the highest enlightenment.

Happiness is seductive. All things considered, for a significant number of us, our interest in Raja YOGA was motivated by the wish to be glad. With ananda samadhi, we appear to have attained our objective. We might be enticed to discontinue our endeavors toward Self-realization. This samadhi doesn't make us immune to ignorance. We are not yet totally free.

Pure I-am-ness

Asmita is the self image sense. In this samadhi, the self image sense itself is the item. This is the highest samprajnata samadhi. There is just awareness of individuality, simply the feeling or thought of "I," or "I-ness." It is simply awareness of one's existence.

The samprajnata samadhis are a procedure of tracing the manifestations of Prakriti back to their source. By going inward, we turn around the pages of evolution. The self image makes the mind. The mind is the reason for the unobtrusive components, which in turn are the basis for the gross components.

Noncognitive (asamprajnata) samadhi happens with the cessation of all conscious idea; just the subconscious impressions remain.

Asamprajnata: asam, "without," and prajna, "information," giving "without information," or a, "not," and samprajnata, giving "not samprajnata" samadhi (the "other" samadhi).

Asamprajnata samadhi is noncognitive on the grounds that there are no items in the conscious mind to discern; even the inner self is temporarily rose above. In spite of the fact that the conscious mind turns out to be totally still, the subconscious impressions (samskaras) remain. Asamprajnata samadhi is the experience of the reflection of the Purusha on a splendidly still, clear mind.

The means from samprajnata to asamprajnata samadhis are:

- First you get Nature (gross and unobtrusive components; the mind and sense of self)
- Then bring it under your influence
- Finally, you rise above it by freeing the mind of all psychological activity. Just subconscious impressions remain

The yogi can't be liberated from the self image until the samskaras are risen above. Samskaras are leftovers of past experiences that help sustain vritti activity by maintaining the structure of the self image. To come to the highest samadhi, nirbija samadhi, even the samskaras should be wiped out. Sri Patanjali addresses nirbija samadhi in the last sutra of this pada.

Yogis who have not attained asamprajnata samadhi remain joined to Prakriti at the time of death because of the continued existence of considerations of becoming.

This scantily worded sutra (the original Sanskrit is just five words) can be interpreted in a few valid and helpful ways, all of which exhibit the same underlying principle: the continued existence of ignorance is the thing that keeps the seeker from advancing to asamprajnata samadhi.

In samprajnata samadhi, the mind has entered to the foundation of issue, to the pure mind, lastly, to the self image, the feeling of "I" itself. However the influence of ignorance over mental functioning remains. The "prospect of becoming" is the persistent desire to experience sense objects manifested from Prakriti. This desire, if not rose above in life, persists significantly subsequent to passing from the physical body. The "prospect of becoming" stops with the attainment of asamprajnata samadhi, the state in which "all conscious idea halts and just the subconscious impressions remain."

To the others, asamprajnata samadhi is gone before by faith, quality, mindfulness, (cognitive) samadhi, and discriminative insight.

"To the others" alludes to those seekers whose progress is not slowed down by the "possibility of becoming."

Faith

We look to faith to sustain us through difficulties and to provide meaning even in trying situations. Faith is not simply a higher type of belief. It is not an amazing wish for something to be valid. Faith is a condition of certainty; of knowing. It is identified with direct perception.

Putting our finger in ice water produces sensations of cold. We state with full faith that the water is cold. Looking out my window, I see that it is raining, and I have faith in what my faculties report to me. In any case, consider this example: I wake up, take a psychological inventory of my wellbeing, and reason that I am fine. I have plentiful vitality and no throbs or pains. However, soon thereafter, I am surprised when my PCP finds that my circulatory strain is high to such an extent that I have to take medication to control it. What turned out badly with my direct perception?

My mind was not consistent or clear enough to make the best possible evaluation; it was insufficient to the assignment. My mind's appraisal was verified incorrect by an instrument equipped for detecting unobtrusive physiological states, a circulatory strain check.

Seekers hope to experience the wellspring of life, the quintessence of all things: God. They may experience sensations or considerations in supplication, worship, and meditation that persuade that what's going on is heavenly, that their belief in God is being confirmed. Yet, how might they be certain? In the above example, our perceptive forces couldn't distinguish hypertension, despite the fact that it existed. Our mind can be tricked in numerous manners.

Numerous years back, there lived a simple, illiterate man whose activity was to ring the sanctuary chimes before sunrise as a call to worship. He had unfailingly dispatched this responsibility since he was a little youngster.

It so happened that one day he became too ill to even think about going to work. He was at home recuperating in bed when out of nowhere he became agitated. His wife raced to his bedside.

"What is it, dear spouse, what disturbs you so?"

"This is terrible, what are we to do? I am too sick to even think about ringing the sanctuary chimes tomorrow first thing."

"Truly, this is along these lines, my better half. Be that as it may, the specialist said that in a couple of days you will be alright to continue with your duties."

"Don't you get it? If I can't ring the chimes, the sun will not rise."

He had linked the chime ringing with the rising of the sun. He had no recollection of a sunrise that was not gone before by his chime ringing. He had faith, however it depended on a blunder. That kind of mistake is anything but difficult to make: we act, experience a reaction, and believe that the action and reaction are linked. Most likely all reactions are linked to a previous action, yet the difficulty lies in deciphering which cause(s) produced which impact. Beliefs should be tested by the rigors of regular daily existence. The chime ringer had the option to cling to a mistaken belief for a long time since it had never been tested. His illness was an opportunity for him to test his faith.

Most items of faith begin as conditional and should be confirmed through the tests that life brings. The word convinced gives a hint to this reality. It intends to be "very much won." Spiritually, to be convinced is to gauge our beliefs and inner experiences against the occasions, difficulties, and sufferings that come our direction.

As faith develops, it brings steadiness of mind. It provides the psychological "room" for life's exercises to be educated. Faith turns into the setting in which we experience occasions. The outcome is that life is not experienced as a series of occasions without purpose however as a significantly rich, inconspicuous, and complex field for learning and development.

Faith is cultivated when we think of the considerable number of blessings we have just received in our lives. This assists with developing gratitude, gratitude ripens into devotion, and devotion culminates in faith.

Strength

The objective of YOGA is difficult to attain. It requires dedication, resolve, and tirelessness to ace the mind.

Strength is a foundation of everything and commitments and is required for accomplishment in any activity or endeavor.

At whatever point we make resolutions, it appears we are tried. Temptations, distractions, and old habits spring up from each side. We have to find the inner strength to endure and to discover approaches to succeed. If we finish the assessments, we will be living heroic lives, demonstrating strength and integrity in our undertakings.

Strength is likewise what sees us through the dry periods of our practices. It is anything but difficult to meditate, ask, and do pranayama when sweet benefits are experienced. Be that as it may, what props us up when we implore and feel nobody is listening or meditate and invest the energy half sleeping or wondering what we ought to have for breakfast?

Each seeker experiences difficult times. What once appeared to be rational currently appears to be foolish. "For what reason would it be advisable for me to be nonattached? I don't appear to get any benefits or having any good times. Furthermore, for what reason would it be a good idea for me to put in several hours daily meditating? I am by all accounts missing out on a great deal of enjoyment in life."

In times of trials we continue simply on the grounds

that we said we would. Our practice does not depend on how we feel however on adhering to principles. That is strength, and it is beautiful.

Mindfulness

Mindfulness (smriti) includes remembering our mistakes, their results, and the exercises learned. It additionally implies being vigilant—maintaining alertness and center in everything we do.

Mindfulness cultivates strength and faith.

Cognitive Samadhi

Samprajnata samadhi is a preparation for asamprajnata samadhi.

Discriminative Insight

Discriminative insight (prajna) is the intuitive information important to arrive at higher conditions of samadhi through continuous mindfulness.

To the sharp and intent practitioner this samadhi comes quickly.

Accomplishment in YOGA comes all the more easily to the individuals who have the richness of youth. Young people have a fearlessness—a willingness to investigate and experience obscure everyday issues. They believe that if they invest sufficient effort, they can achieve any objective. As we get more established, we discover that we can't have everything we strive for—and that is a piece of maturing. In any case, in that procedure, we sometimes lose the willing vitality of youth. Certainly, we should look before we jump, however once the decision to jump is made, it ought to be done wholeheartedly. Seekers who dive within themselves with vigor and energy attain results sooner. Achievement breeds considerably more noteworthy inspiration and enthusiasm. If we are engaged, inspired, dedicated, unafraid of difficulties, and continually seeking to develop and learn, we will gain ground quickly.

A sincere understudy once moved toward his master with a question: "Ace, I have been meditating and practicing a wide range of disciplines for a long time. Still, I have not seen God. What is fundamental for me to do? What am I missing?"

Instead of speaking, the ace accompanied his young understudy to the banks of a close by river. He requested that he twist around. Abruptly he got a handle on the youngster by the rear of the neck and push his head submerged.

Before long the man was squirming, struggling to break free. A couple of long minutes went before he was discharged.

Gasping for air, he asked, "Ace, for what reason did you do this to me?" "When your head was submerged, what were you thinking?" "I was just thinking of breathing. Nothing else."

"You didn't think of your wife, your activity, your finances?" "No, just getting air to relax."

"At the point when you think of God with the same one-pointed intensity, realize that the experience of Him is exceptionally close within reach."

Practitioners who place the highest incentive on activities that advance their spiritual advancement realize samadhi more quickly than understudies with a tepid attitude.

The time fundamental for progress likewise relies upon whether the practice is mild, moderate, or intense.

The previous sutra talked about the enthusiasm of the practitioner. This sutra develops the idea of the intensity, the quantity of practices per-shaped and how much they are integrated into daily life. The more practices that are incorporated into daily life, the sooner the influence of ignorance diminishes.

A mild practice describes one that needs consistent enthusiasm and is probably irregular. For these understudies, practice is minimal and viewed as an important errand. Practitioners in the middle classification normally find probably some time ordinarily to fit in YOGA practices. They enjoy benefits, yet a lot of their practice remains disconnected from the remainder of their lives. Fanatical practitioners make sadhana their priority. They keep inspired and centered and anticipate periods of practice. They likewise will in general consider each to be of their lives as an opportunity for development. For them, practice turns into a character trait.

In spite of the fact that accomplishment in YOGA requires full application of our assets, we ought to be prepared for fanaticism. Any practice or lifestyle that deserts equalization and congruity can prompt lopsided improvement, rigidity of viewpoint, and interpersonal strife. Practice ought to be adjusted by nonattachment.

Chapter 9: How to Attain Samadhi with Devotion and Total Dedication to God (Ishwara)

So far, the emphasis has been on practices that work directly with the modifications in the mind by redirecting or holding attention. Here we find another way to Self-realization. Devotion (pranidhana), interpreted literally, signifies "to place or hold in front." It implies giving prime importance to the dedication of our time, capabilities, and vitality to God. To put it plainly, this sutra presents sacrificial love of God as a legitimate way to Self-realization. Our minds normally harp on that which we love. In common relationships, when we love somebody we can't quit thinking about them. We anticipate seeing them, talking to them, pleasing and serving them. There is nothing we would prefer to accomplish more than be with our darling. It is the same with affection for God. The individuals who have a loving, gave attitude toward God find that the selective focal point of nirodha is easier to attain, and in light of the fact that loving is fun, it is increasingly enjoyable. Regularity and enthusiasm are additionally more easily attained. Obviously, there are favorable circumstances that go to devotion to Ishwara. Be that as it may, who or what is Ishwara?

Ishwara is derived from ish, "to administer or possess," and can be thought of as the Supreme Ruler of Creation. It is the Purusha as experienced from within the confines of Prakriti and perceived through the limitations of the inner self. Ishwara is not discrete from Purusha (Self), yet is a method for externalizing It.

The externalization of the Self is common propensity. It is a piece of a learning procedure. When grappling with unpretentious certainties, we search for images that assist us with understanding the subtleties of those facts. In Christianity, for example, a three-leafed clover is utilized to symbolize the puzzle of the trinity: how the one God could likewise be three separate personalities, Father, Son, and Holy Spirit. Instead of contemplating complex theological contentions that endeavor to reconcile this principle, we could draw analogies with the three leaves on one stem. Similarly, it is difficult to get a handle on surrendering to the indefinable, infinite Self. Externalizing the Self as Ishwara offers something for the mind to get a handle on onto. A one-pointed, dedicated relationship with Ishwara permits love and affection to develop. From this, give up follows.

This sutra addresses endless enthusiasts who are dedicated to their faith and who sincerely worship, supplicate, and go to chapel, synagogue, or sanctuary. They don't have to find out about mantras, Prakriti, buddhi, or vrittis to achieve liberation. What they are doing is sufficient. To adore and be given to God in any structure is a valid way in Raja YOGA. The impetus for development is simply the total giving to worship, devotion, and service. One reason that loving devotion is highly esteemed as a spiritual practice is on the grounds that it is the most ideal approach to beat dread.

Dread is one of the most settled in impediments that YOGA practitioners experience. Dread is the means by which the sense of self reacts when it perceives its existence is compromised. The personality calls itself "I," so its dissolution is experienced as "I am dying."

Whenever it is in a powerless position, the "I" reasserts itself due to the dread of extinction. Since the personality remains between the seeker and Self-realization, ignorance continues.

Dread can be overwhelmed by the will, yet for the greater part of us, it is all the more easily accomplished through adoration, which normally dissipates dread. For the sweetheart, nothing is more regular or desirable than union with the dearest. What begins as the respectful devotion of the seeker to Ishwara progressively develops to an adoration so consuming that the dread of self-extinction is survived.

Overcoming the dread of self-extinction is sufficiently daunting, yet the fear is exasperated when we endeavor to give up to a Reality without name, structure, or quality. It is like leaping into a tremendous obscure. We don't have anything familiar or inspiring on which we can pour our attention. We need to beat a profound situated dread when attempting to submit to an Infinite Cosmic Principle whose face can't be seen and who is devoid of any recognizable characteristics.

Then again, it is a lot easier to imagine giving ourselves to the One:

- Who is the supreme Purusha, unaffected by any afflictions, actions, or fruits of actions or by any inner impressions
- Who is unconditioned by time and the instructor of the most ancient educators
- In whom there is the finished manifestation of the seed of omniscience

- Who is unchanging
- Who, when experienced, brings the seeker spiritual independence and complete rest

These characteristics of Ishwara are methods for describing a portion of the experiences seekers can expect as they draw nearer to realization of the Self.

Raja YOGA doesn't require choosing between the will or loving give up. For most, it is smarter to exercise the two capacities, however the emphasis will shift according to the individual.

Experience It

Give up is the active side of faith. Opportunities to cultivate it happen when our beliefs meet realties that differ from our conceptions or expectations. Give up can't be constrained; it is the result of a vision of life dependent on trusting that there is divine wisdom behind all occasions. In any case, it is a mind-set that can be cultivated through dedicating the fruits of actions to God and by the practice of acceptance.

Dedication. We know from studying nonattachment that actions motivated by selfish expectations bring pain. One method for overcoming selfish expectations is to take part in actions yet dedicate the fruits of those actions to God. Dedication changes ordinary actions into amazing spiritual practices.

Acceptance. The entire creation exists to give the experiences fundamental for the liberation of the Purusha. Our regular experience discloses to us that our intents and actions can't necessarily change the course of history—individual, familial, societal, or worldwide. We create acceptance each time we remind ourselves that regardless of what happens, it ultimately brings about our spiritual unfoldment.

With acceptance, there are no expectations or requests put on anything to change or to comply with our own conception of how life ought to be. Acceptance is trust in Ishwara (the Supreme Ruler) to direct the universe wisely.

Ishwara is the supreme Purusha, unaffected by any afflictions, actions, fruits of actions, or any inner impressions of desires.

How are we to identify with God?

The sutra alludes to Ishwara as the "supreme Purusha." Meanings for "purusha" include spirit, individual soul, or individual. It is a word that is normally utilized when referring to any individual. We are all purushas, however Ishwara is the supreme one, since He/She/It is liberated from subconscious impressions and not influenced by any afflictions or karma. As it were, Ishwara is much the same as us, however without ignorance and its outcomes. Obviously, the equation read from the opposite side is that we are Ishwara, limited (evidently) by ignorance.

In Ishwara is the finished manifestation of the seed of omniscience.

This emphasizes the worthiness of Ishwara as an object of worship. This sutra can likewise show us something of the relationship among finite and infinite and fill in as a proof for the existence of the Infinite. There can't be finite without infinite. Close your eyes and picture a circle. What do you see around it? Blackness. Where does the blackness end? It doesn't. Make the circle bigger. What is there around it? More blackness. Where does this blackness end? It doesn't end. Etc. All considerations, realities, guesses, and aspirations are finite realities anticipated upon the infinite omniscient screen that is Ishwara. The limited self can be known in light of the fact that it shows up against an omniscient scenery.

Unconditioned by time, Ishwara is the instructor of even the most ancient educators

In the previous sutra, we discovered that Ishwara knows it all there is to know. Presently we discover something of the idea of Divine information. This precious information is not to be spared, like assets in a protected deposit box. It fulfills its destiny just when communicated to the individuals who need it. Similarly, as it is our inclination to look for information, it is Ishwara's tendency to share it.

"Unconditioned by time" implies that Ishwara's infinite storage facility of information and wisdom is unceasingly present and constantly accessible. The information that was available to the yogis of yesterday continues to be available today and will continue to be available for an infinite number of tomorrows.

The wording of this sutra is significant for another explanation. We are not informed that Ishwara is the wellspring of information. Instead, Ishwara is characterized as the educator (literally, master) of instructors. "Guru" likely held significance for understudies who lived in a culture with a since a long time ago established tradition of receiving spiritual information through the guidance of a qualified instructor. For them, seeking direction from an ace was presumably as regular as getting the climate forecast from the TV is for us.

Just a lit flame can light an unlit one. Since time immemorial, the same sparkle of information continues to be passed from educator to understudy.

We live in times when numerous YOGA understudies question the necessity of studying under an ace. Our way of life puts a high incentive on confidence and prizes the ability of the individual to reason through issues on his or her own. Our fascination with confidence is exhibited by book shop retires that are packed with self improvement guides and the numerous TV and radio television shows that normally include self improvement portions. In spite of the fact that we try to act naturally reliant, we additionally appear to consistently be looking for somebody to tell us the best way to be so.

In such an environment, YOGA understudies might presume that they can effectively practice YOGA without an instructor. In spite of the fact that this might be possible with the physical practices of Hatha YOGA or to begin practicing meditation, the way of self improvement is not appropriate to the unpretentious, difficult, and delicate undertaking of cleaning the inner self of ignorance. Around there, our objectivity will regularly be slanted. A skilled third gathering to guide and instruct us is invaluable. All things considered, extraordinary ballet artists go to ace classes (the further developed they are, the more important this is). Accomplished competitors appreciate their mentors' daily observation and corrections. Thousands go to gyms to exercise under according to a trainer. The basic principle is simple and sound: utilize the individuals who have ventured to every part of the street before us. They right our mistakes and help us to avoid wrong turns.

Despite the fact that information on the Self is within us, it should be called forward. Somewhat, we can experience this calling forward of information through books, tapes, and classes. Be that as it may, it is all the more quickly and totally stirred within the setting of an ace/disciple relationship. The disciple finds in the ace the fulfillment of spiritual potential. Enlightenment turns out to be genuine—a possibility within arrive at that fills the disciple with inspiration, expectation, and challenge.

A decent disciple ought to be available to learning something new as well as prepared to relinquish or change previous conceptions. Receptivity depends on humility, accepting that we don't know it all and that there is a lot to discover that would benefit us.

There is another important principle grinding away in the ace/disciple relationship that we ought to investigate: emulation.

Each and every League mentor knows the intensity of emulation. When small kids go to their first practice, they as of now have a considerable lot of the skills they will convey with them all through their playing years, even to the significant league level. They attained this high level of skill at such a youthful age by watching their legends on TV and emulating them.

They bat, toss, and run like their favorite player, learning exquisitely inconspicuous techniques that would take a mentor a very long time to instruct. Obviously, they pick up certain habits that however not necessarily destructive, are not vital for progress. Perhaps they will imitate their legends' facial expressions or the manner in which they contact their protective cap before stepping into the player's crate. A considerable lot of these superfluous habits fall away, and the understudies will create refinements and progressions all alone or with the assistance of their mentors. Emulation is normal, simple, and incredibly amazing. YOGA understudies imitate their lord and, in that emulation, learn more than words alone can pass on.

Emulation is one of the principles behind apprenticeship. It is the technique for concentrate generally esteemed by the individuals who are progressed in their field. Where do propelled pianists go to refine their skills further? They concentrate under the vigilant gaze of somebody they feel has accomplished what they look for. The same is valid in spiritual issues. Find somebody in whom you have faith, who you feel has experienced the objective of YOGA. If that is impractical, it is still worthwhile to concentrate under somebody who is at any rate a couple of strides in front of you. Wisdom passing starting with one individual then onto the next is like being kissed by the Truth. It is beautiful and ground-breaking.

The expression of Ishwara is the mystic sound OM.

This sutra introduces us to the mantra OM, which means Ishwara. In the Sanskrit, "OM" isn't mentioned. Instead, we find the term, pranavah, the humming of prana. OM is the murmur of the business of Creation: the making, evolving, and dissolving of beings and articles. You can hear it in the thunder of a fire, the profound thunder of the sea, or the ground-shaking surge of a tornado's winds. Since the pranavah is not something we can easily recite, the name is given as OM. It is continually vibrating within us, replaying the drama of creation, evolution, and dis-solution on numerous levels. This murmur can be heard in profound meditation, when outer sound is risen above and internal gab stilled.

The identity of primordial sound with God as the creative power of the universe is not limited to Raja YOGA. It is a principle found in numerous spiritual traditions. The Bible proclaims, "In the beginning was the Word, and the Word was with God and the Word was God" (John 1.1). The Rig Veda, one of the most ancient scriptures on the planet, contains a similar entry: "In the beginning was Brahman (God) and with Brahman was sabda (primordial sound) and sabda was really the Supreme Brahman."

Since the utilization of mantras is a focal practice in numerous schools of YOGA, it will be valuable to examine them in a little detail.

Mantras

Mantras (literally, to secure the mind) are sound syllables representing parts of the Divine. They are not simply fabricated words utilized as names for objects. They are not part of the language in that capacity. They are the inconspicuous vibratory substance of things, introduced as sounds that can be rehashed. Concentrated repetition of a mantra shapes the basis of an entire part of YOGA: Japa YOGA, the YOGA of Repetition.

Sounds can mitigate or agitate us. Numerous individuals shiver when they hear a metal utensil scratch the base of a metal skillet. At the same time, incalculable vacationers search out the shoreline in request to lie back and let the sound of the waves relieve their worn out nerves. Mantras are sounds that quiet and fortify the mind, and consequently they are ideally suited to fill in as objects of meditation. The vibratory intensity of the mantra improves the meditative experience.

When a mantra has been picked, practitioners by and large gain the best ground if they stick to it forever. Understudies may pick a mantra themselves dependent on trial and mistake or in light of the fact that it is associated with a particular deity with whom they feel a solid connection. For example, OM Namah Sivaya is a mantra associated with Lord Siva. Be that as it may, since the word siva speaks to auspiciousness, the repetition of this mantra is not restricted to lovers of Lord Siva. Mantras rise above these designations. They are sound equations whose fundamental benefit derives from their vibration, not associated ideas or images.

A few understudies receive a mantra from an ace or adroit in whom they have faith. For this situation, they put their faith in the educator to decide for them. The understudy is still making the essential choice in the two scenarios. The difference is that in the previous, the understudy picks the mantra; in the last mentioned, the understudy picks the educator who chooses the mantra.

Japa YOGA is not limited to Sanskrit and Raja YOGA. Repetition of amazing sounds and petitions—Shalom, Maranatha, and Ave Maria, for example—is utilized in numerous spiritual traditions.

OM

The word "OM" is been used to signify Ishwara should be special; it ought to be liberated from the limitations of time, circumstance, or faith tradition. Not exclusively should this designation be universal, it should likewise bring the experience of Ishwara to the practitioner. Sri Patanjali states that the name that accomplishes this is OM.

OM is the origin all things considered. It comprises three letters: A, U, and M (OM rhymes with "home" since the A and U, when combined, become a long O sound). An is the first solid. You simply open your mouth and make a sound. All audible sound begins with this action. It speaks to creation. The U is framed when the sound moves forward toward the lips with the assistance of the tongue and cheeks. This speaks to evolution. Finally, to make the M sound the lips meet up. This last stable speaks to dissolution. So together A, U, and M signify creation, evolution, and dissolution. The entire pattern of life is spoken to in these three letters.

According to the philosophy of Advaita Vedanta (the philosophical school of nondualism), An is external consciousness, U is inner con-sciousness, and M is superconsciousness. The same three letters additionally signify the waking, dreaming, and profound dreamless rest states. Past these three states is a fourth express, the Absolute, the silence that rises above all limitations.

In spite of the fact that there are numerous mantras, the wellspring of all mantras is OM. A portion of the more widely realized mantras include OM Shanti, Hari OM, OM Namah Sivaya, and OM Mani Padme Hum. Most yet not all mantras utilized for meditation contain OM.

Considering its symbolism and force, it is reasonable why Sri Patanjali identifies OM as the "name" for Ishwara.

Universality of OM

Sri Swami Satchidananda's discourse on this sutra says:

We ought to comprehend that OM was not invented by anyone. A few people didn't meet up, hold nominations, take a vote, and the majority decided, "Good, let God have the name OM." No. He Himself manifested as OM. Any seeker who truly needs to see God eye to eye will ultimately consider Him to be OM. That is the reason it rises above all geographical, political, or theological limitations. It doesn't have a place with one nation or one religion; it has a place with the entire universe.

It is a variation of this OM that we see as the "Amen" or "Ameen," which the Christians, Muslims, and Jews state. That doesn't mean somebody transformed it. Truth is consistently the same. Any place you sit for meditation, you will ultimately end in experiencing OM or the murmur. However, when you need to communicate what you experienced, you may utilize different words according to your capacity or the language you know.

To rehash it in a meditative manner uncovers its meaning.

The two watchwords in this sutra are artha and bhavanam:

- Artha signifies meaning, reason, or aim; from the root "arth," to point out.
- Bhavanam's meanings include meditation, consideration, disposition, feeling, and mental discipline.

A few parts of Hindu philosophy comprehend bhavana as a particular disposition of mind—one in which things are continually practiced or recollected. Mantra repetition is not the mindless parroting of a sound but rather an attentive and informed act set against a foundation of enthusiasm. Consistent mental concentration and an understanding of the significance of the mantra are required. In this manner the meaning (or reason for) the mantra will bit by bit unfurl. This understanding is in agreement with one of Raja YOGA's basic precepts: centered attention brings about more profound and subtler perceptions.

For sharp seekers, every single repetition is a snapshot of connection with the Self, an affirmation of the Truth of their own spiritual identity, and a reminder of their intentions.

From this practice, the awareness turns inward, and the distracting snags vanish.

At the point when the mind "tunes in" to the vibration of OM, it gets introspective and begins to stir to Self-information. Meanwhile, the distracting obstructions, which are the result of a dissipated mind, normally dissolve.

By extension, we could claim a similar benefit for the repetition of any mantra and for the practice of meditation when all is said in done.

This sutra introduces a key topic in Raja YOGA: the practices don't directly bring spiritual advancement; they simply evacuate snags that forestall it. The evolution of the individual normally happens when that which hinders its advancement is expelled.

- They [accepting pain as help for purification, study, and surrender] assist us with minimizing deterrents and attain samadhi.
- By the practice of the limbs of YOGA, the impurities dwindle away and there day breaks the light of wisdom, leading to discriminative discernment.
- Incidental occasions don't directly cause common evolution; they simply expel the obstructions as a rancher [removes hindrances in a water course running to his field].

Chapter 10: Distractions and Obstacles

Disease, dullness, question, carelessness, laziness, sensuality, bogus perception, failure to arrive at firm ground, and slipping starting from the earliest stage—these distractions of the mind-stuff are the impediments.

This list of impediments will be familiar to the individuals who have been practicing YOGA for any period of time. Each seeker faces them at various points on their spiritual excursion.

Vikshepa, deciphered as "distraction," implies bogus projection, scattering, dispersing, and shaking (of the mind-stuff). Vikshepa recommends that the hindrances are manifestations of a need or loss of core interest. It is interesting to take note of that misperception is additionally conceived of absence of consistent mental core interest. Again and again, we see why nirodha—the ability to attain an unmistakable centered mind—is the foundation of spiritual life.

The deterrents structure a kind of chain reaction, one leading to the following.

Disease

This represents any physical discomfort or disorder that keeps us from completely engaging in YOGA practices. It can present as any number of diverse issues, for example, fatigue, aching lower back when sitting for meditation, nagging allergies, or continuous cerebral pains. Whatever the explanation, the understudy's practice gets irregular because of the test of physical distress.

Weakness

What is the aftereffect of irregular practice? Very little advancement is made. It's difficult to be sharp and intent if you don't experience anything nice in your practices. The mind begins to make some hard memories focusing. Nirodha begins to appear to be an impossible dream. The final product is dullness of mind.

At the point when the mind can't center, it can't infiltrate into the more profound meaning of things. This being along these lines, the following stage normally follows....

Uncertainty

"I don't have the foggiest idea. These teachings are terribly intense. What's more, they appear to be excessively idealistic. Or on the other hand possibly I don't have the ability for this. I'm additionally starting to think about whether possibly my instructor doesn't have a clue about what's truly best for me."

We question the veracity or practicality of the teachings or, considerably progressively inconvenient, we question ourselves. We have not gained the ground we figured we would. We feel a bit let down. Our hearts are not in our practice like previously. Our normal practice currently includes another factor: uncertainty.

Uncertainty can be a serious impediment to advance. At the point when our practice has slowed down because of uncertainty, our first obligation is to have the questions cleared. Pose inquiries of adepts and experts; read and study more; take the necessary steps to expel the uncertainties from your heart.

Obviously, question, in addition to being its own difficult deterrent, adds fuel to dullness.

Carelessness

Despite the fact that the first three deterrents are working their spell, being a decent understudy, you drive forward. Be that as it may, there's very little enthusiasm.

The vitality of the mind is torn by question and dissipated by disease and dullness. It is characteristic that such a practice be set apart via carelessness. You scarcely focus on your practices.

"Did I simply inhale or hold my breath? What round am I doing?" The finish of your meditation session comes, and you have no clue what you've been doing for as long as thirty minutes—likely not repeating your mantra.

In addition to the fact that you cease experiencing progress, however whatever energy and profundity your practice had are slipping ceaselessly.

Laziness

YOGA practice presently turns out to be nothing in excess of an errand. Do you want to practice any longer? Not likely. You become apathetic as to your practices.

Master Buddha encouraged that the main sin was laziness. If we don't endeavor to better ourselves, by what method can there be promise for accomplishment in YOGA?

Sensuality

The mind is exhausted, and an exhausted mind consistently searches for a distraction—another amusement or something to do. It gets mischievous. If it can't find anything satisfying within the practices, it will hope to gratify the faculties.

The Sanskrit word for sensuality, avirati, additionally signifies "to dissipate" and alludes to the dissipation of our vitality that comes when the mind loses its concentration and resolve and tries to satisfy sexy cravings. The reduction in the vitality intensifies the various hindrances.

Bogus Perception

"Truly, I used to practice Raja YOGA. Try not to misunderstand me, a few parts of YOGA are acceptable, however these Eastern philosophies miss the point. All things considered, shouldn't I live life with energy, wringing out each drop of fun I can? What's more, those yogis lived such a long time ago! Patanjali couldn't have anticipated the present world. Or then again perhaps he simply didn't confront life for what it's worth. It appears that YOGA is extremely about the suppression of common impulses and emotions. I wonder how different these sutras would be if Patanjali were alive today."

What appeared to be so obviously valid in the beginning presently appears to be withdrawn. We may begin to believe that our evaluation of YOGA as meaningful for our lives was a mistake. Most practices are deserted, with the exception of maybe a couple of pressure relieving techniques.

Bogus perception is significant among the obstructions since it most looks like ignorance

Failing to Attain Firm Ground

It is difficult to gain ground when the practices and attainments have not gotten firmly grounded, an integral piece of how we experience life. Another approach to comprehend this hindrance is that it is the inability to attain or maintain centered attention.

Slipping from the Ground Reached

Slipping starting from the earliest stage can happen in light of the fact that we fall again into to destructive habits, or because of broadened periods of physical or emotional pressure, or even on the grounds that in the wake of making a little advancement, we get a little self-satisfied and "settle for the status quo." Whatever the explanation, it is a typical experience to lose, at any rate temporarily, a portion of the spiritual advancement we have made.

It is discouraging to buckle down, gain some ground, and afterward slip back. It can feel like Dante's vision of hades, where poor spirits consume enormous vitality to creep out of an immense, burning pit, just to fall again into the flames at the brink of break.

If these snags are left unchecked, we will lose a lot of what we have gained. The assurance of failing to fall back arrives just with the highest samadhi. However for those of us who have done a lot of slipping, it is reassuring that Sri Patanjali comprehends our plight. He realizes this occurs and has given us two amazing remedies

It is anything but difficult to become discouraged when we experience these obstructions. We ought to remind ourselves that encountering hindrances is regular. Instead of becoming discouraged or worried, we can accept the open door to search inside and see what exercises the snags can educate us.

There is a story that shows the tricky way obstructions can slip into our lives and distract us from our intentions. Not all the deterrents are spoken to in this story, yet you will recognize a couple of the key ones and the slippery incline they present.

There used to be a youthful yogi who had lived at his master's ashram for various years. He was a dedicated disciple who practiced with extraordinary enthusiasm. At some point, he noticed his lord looking at him in a curious manner.

"Ace, is there something incorrectly? You are looking at me in the most peculiar manner."

"No, nothing is off-base. Yet, as I was watching you, it happened to me that it would be beneficial for you to experience a period of seclusion to concentrate on deepening your meditation."

"Fine, ace. I'm glad to do as you state."

"Great. A couple of miles from here there is a nice settlement with a little village close by where you can proceed to ask for your daily nourishment. Remain there until I seek you."

"It sounds great. I'll go on the double."

Following his lord's instructions, he took just a begging bowl and two loincloths. Arriving at the bank of a stream, he found a raised spot where he built his hovel.

He at that point started a routine that was rehashed faithfully for a long time; in the wake of morning meditation, he would take one loincloth, wash it, wrap it on the top of his hovel to dry, and afterward stroll to the village to ask for nourishment.

At that point one day, when he came back to the hovel he noticed that a rodent had eaten an opening in his loincloth. What to do? The following day, he asked for nourishment and another loincloth. The villagers were very much glad to support him. Tragically, the rodent would not leave and continued ruining one loincloth after another. One villager showed compassion for him.

"Child, look how much difficulty that rodent is causing you. Regular you need to ask for nourishment and furthermore for another loincloth. What you need is a feline to ward off the rodent."

The youngster was paralyzed at the simple logic of the appropriate response. That very day he asked for nourishment, a loincloth, and a feline. He obtained a nice kitten.

Be that as it may, things did not go as he anticipated. In spite of the fact that the feline did ward off the rodent, it, as well, required nourishment. Presently he needed to ask for a bowl of milk for his feline just as nourishment for himself. This continued for half a month, until...

"Youngster, I noticed you begging for nourishment for yourself and milk for your feline. Why not get a cow? Not exclusively would you be able to take care of the feline, you'll even have milk left over for yourself!"

He thought this was brilliant. It required some investment, yet he had the option to find a villager to give him a bovine. At this point, you may have thought about what occurs straightaway. While the milk from the cow took care of his feline and provided some milk for him, it too expected to even consider eating. Presently, when he asked for nourishment, he additionally needed to request feed for the cow. After some time...

"Dear kid, what a weight it is to ask for nourishment and feed for your dairy animals, as well! Simply do one simple thing and every one of your issues will be finished. You are living on fertile soil. Ask for hayseed and plant roughage to take care of the dairy animals. You will certainly have enough feed left over to sell in town. With the additional cash you could purchase whatever you need."

The youthful disciple considered how he could have missed such a simple solution. He discovered hayseed to plant and before long gathered a rich yield of feed. In any case, one day a villager spotted him, looking run down.

"Child, you are working excessively hard. You have a growing business to take care of. What you need is a wife to impart responsibilities to you. Later on, your children will likewise have the option to help.

Obviously, he thought. So simple. He did find a nice lady to wed. His business and family developed significantly. Truth be told, his cottage was before long supplanted by a mansion set up with hirelings.

One day there was a thump at the entryway.

The youngster strolled to the entryway and investigated the eyes of his lord. An unexpected surge of recognition brought back memories of since a long time ago overlooked and ignored commitments. Looking heavenward, he raised his arms high and yelled. . .

"Just for the need of a loincloth!"

The good is not: don't have pets, a business, or a

companion; it's: generally watch out for your objective. It is too simple to even consider slipping starting from the earliest stage.

Accompaniments to the psychological distractions include dis-tress, despair, trembling of the body, and disturbed breathing.

In life, the deterrents don't necessarily appear to us as introduced in the previous sutra. Very few practitioners have felt, "I am experiencing bogus perception nowadays." The snags are like viruses. We can't directly perceive their essence in our frameworks. We have to figure out how to recognize the side effects. This sutra presents the main manifestations of the obstructions.

The concentration on a single subject (or the utilization of one technique) is the most ideal approach to forestall the deterrents and their accompaniments.

Meditation can be viewed as the best approach to defeat impediments; here we discover that commitment is the preventive against future events. Steadiness of mind is the basis for the two remedies, manifesting as engaged attention in meditation and diligence in life.

There is a story that exhibits the intensity of sticking to a certain something. It begins with a little youngster's first day of school.

The educator invited the class energetically.

"Today is a special day: your absolute first day of school. We will regard this day as a holiday. I will send you home early, yet simply subsequent to teaching you something that you can show your folks."

In any event in the beginning, most understudies anticipate going home to exhibit what they realized in school that day.

"Class, today we will figure out how to write the main."

The class was thrilled. The instructor went to the writing board and with the chalk followed the single stroke for all the class to see.

"Presently all of you attempt it."

Individually, she checked all the understudies' papers.

"Great. Great. Fine. Extremely nice. Class, you have all done quite well, you are dismissed for now."

The following day, the educator gave another assignment.

"Young men and girls, you did so well yesterday that we can continue to number two." She drew the sample on the board for all to see. Again, she walked around and down the isles checking the papers.

"Great, Good. Fine. O, child, you more likely than not misunderstood." She was talking to our young saint.

"You are still writing number one, and today we are practicing number two. Your number ones are fine, if it's not too much trouble proceed onward."

"Educator, I realize we are doing number two, however some way or another I don't think I have comprehended the main yet."

"Well . . . OK. I'll let you continue with number one

today, however you should find the class by tomorrow, or you will fall excessively far behind."

The following day the educator composed the number three on the board for the class to duplicate.

"Great. Great. Fine... O, child, you are still practicing number one. Take it from me. I'm a school instructed instructor. Your main is flawlessly satisfactory. There is no purpose behind you to continue practicing it."

"I get, educator. I would prefer not to raise any ruckus; it's simply that I don't feel like I comprehend the main."

The educator didn't know what to do. The kid was otherwise respectful and intelligent. Days passed and the class continued to progress, while our youngster insisted on practicing number one. Finally, in a snapshot of exasperation, the educator lost her temper.

"Get out. Return home. Perhaps your folks can accomplish something with you."

"Alright, instructor. I'm sorry to have been an issue for you."

The kid returned home and explained what had befallen his folks. They were shaken. He had never exhibited any willful behavior. They discussed the situation and trusted that possibly with their adoration and patience they could guide him through this perplexing issue.

Shockingly, the kid continued the same behavior with his folks. Regular they gave their best exertion and ordinary he replied, "I am so sorry to hurt you, Mom and Dad. I don't intend to disobey; it is only that I don't comprehend the main."

Following half a month of this, even the guardians lost their temper. "Escape our sight. Simply go out."

Quietly the kid left, in the long run entering the huge timberland at the edge of their village. Minutes after the fact, the guardians, regretting their upheaval, scanned for their child yet couldn't find him.

At that point one day, the kid showed up at the homeroom. The instructor, excited at this point restrained by the kid's past behavior, simply invited him and afterward included, "Is there anything we can accomplish for you child? Is there anything you need to state?"

"Truly, educator, I currently know the main."

"OK like to come up to the front of the room and show everybody your main?"

"Certainly, if you like."

The little kid serenely strolled to the front of the room. Picking up the chalk and turning to the writing board, he made the simple straight line of the main... and the chalkboard split into equal parts.

The kid's attentive repetition of the main brought about an extraordinary demonstration of the intensity of a one-pointed mind. At the point when he embraced the simple demonstration of tracing a straight line on the board, it took on miraculous dimensions.

We need that kind of one-pointed steadiness to defeat

hindrances and pierce the facade of ignorance. We ought to never give up. Numerous individuals quit when they are on the brink of progress. Determination consistently pays off. Ants, daily walking the same way over a stone divider, will wear a depression in it one day. Likewise, our practices will in the end eradicate ignorance.

By cultivating attitudes of friendliness toward the glad, compassion for the miserable, delight in the virtuous, and equanimity toward the nonvirtuous, the mind-stuff retains its undisturbed calmness.

Chapter 11: Locks and Keys of Life

Sri Patanjali divides interactions into four categories. These are the "locks;" the riddles or difficulties we face daily. The "keys" that are applied to these situations help the mind retain undisturbed calmness. The locks and keys are not prescriptions for specific actions: we are not determined what to do however how to be; the means by which to cultivate attitudes that guarantee that the instrument of perception (the mind) is in the best condition to settle on the best possible evaluations and choices.

Lock 1: Happiness; The Key: Friendliness

We might think it is normal to be friendly toward somebody who is upbeat. Tragically, this is not in every case genuine. There are times when another's happiness (or achievement) reminds us of our failures or unfulfilled desires. In spite of the fact that we may not turn out to be unmistakably irate or discouraged, our well-wishing could be mixed with jealousy or desire. For example, this might occur if a friend receives the promotion we sought after. Our great contemplations could be diminished by lament or jealousy.

Sri Patanjali suggests cultivating friendliness toward the upbeat as the way to undisturbed calmness. We should befriend happiness, find a workable pace, give it legitimate attention and regard. If we harp on happiness, looking for it like a miner's eye looks for gold, we will cultivate it in our lives.

Lock 2: Unhappiness; The Key: Compassion

Sometimes the unhappiness of others feels like a weight. We may get impatient, wondering how our sibling can commit the same error again and again. Maybe we think that he should simply get over his grief and continue ahead with life. There are times when the suffering of others can make us uncomfortable or frightened. In our discomfort, we get some distance from them.

Instead, at whatever point we see unhappiness we should utilize the com-passion key. To be compassionate doesn't necessarily imply that we cry when our sibling cries or become irate in request to help our sister's frustration. In the name of compassion there are times when the appropriate reaction is to deliver a solid piece of advice that is difficult to hear. Be that as it may, behind our actions, we ought to cherish one overriding motive: the government assistance of others. All actions ought to continue from a position of caring and loving.

A compassionate heart is a solace and backing to many. We create compassion by recalling demonstrations of kindness that have benefited us while remembering the pain, alienation, despair, and confusion brought about by suffering.

Compassion requires fortitude and strength: the fearlessness to move past our own interests to associate with the suffering of others, and the strength to help hold up under their suffering.

Lock 3: Virtuous; The Key: Delight

Virtues are good traits, for example, patience, boldness, reliability—that bring benefit to other people and mischief to nobody. They are signs of spiritual maturity and fill in as reliable compasses with which we can navigate the uncertainties of life's choices.

Virtues can be created through investigation and contemplation or, as this sutra proposes, through recognizing their quality in others. As such, we ought to cultivate the habit of celebrating virtues any place we recognize them. The more we rejoice in them, the sooner they will be our own.

This practice is especially helpful in experiences with individuals who make us awkward or whom we don't like. Everybody has probably a few virtues. Is it true that we are perceptive enough to recognize any in our enemies? We might find that behavior we once comprehended as obnoxious might uncover constancy. What we once viewed as pushy currently gives us a glimpse into the benefits of firm convictions.

Lock 4: Nonvirtuous; Key: Equanimity

Upeksha, deciphered as "equanimity," originates from upa, "to go close or toward," and iksha, "to take a gander at or on." with regards to this sutra, we can comprehend it as the ability to obviously perceive the idea of the nonvirtuous demonstration through close and unbiased examination.

Tragic to state, we as a whole over and over again witness or are victims of injustices. This sutra is not promoting aloofness or praising an uncaring attitude. Despite the fact that outrage frequently feels justifiable and sometimes appears the most ideal approach to address an injustice, Sri Patanjali doesn't find it a satisfactory attitude for a yogi to have. Instead, we are tested to accomplish something that may appear to be counterintuitive when we face a nonvirtuous demonstration: keep our equanimity.

In spite of the fact that it's normal to want to strike back when we are victims of somebody's wrongdoing, outrage causes incredible mischief:

- It deprives us of harmony and neutrality of mind.
- Our bodies become unstable and disturbed. Outrage debilitates us physically.
- Anger crushes reason and stifles creativity. The loss of reason and creativity implies that better ways to deal with resolving conflicts are regularly missed.
- Every demonstration of outrage predisposes us to additionally instances. Rehashed actions make

habits; and habits continued structure character: we are at risk for becoming bitter individuals.
- Even if it brings benefit to other people, our annoyance harms us first.

While outrage sometimes motivates individuals to address an injustice, there is a perspective more qualified for dealing with the nonvirtuous. The mind had of equanimity is in the best position to find solutions. It is solid, clear, and liberated from bias.

We needn't bother with outrage to motivate us to make the wisest decision. We can act from higher motives: compassion, the away from of what is right, and the solid wish to bring about concordance. With clarity of mind we will comprehend the wicked demonstration and its implications, increasing the odds of finding creative and effective solutions.

This brings us to a related topic: how, when, and whether we should endeavor to address another who is occupied with nonvirtuous actions. There are occasions when taking corrective action is not the best course. It could even be counterproductive. For example, somebody you care for may not be prepared to hear your accommodating advice concerning some indiscreet habit. They may respond out of resentment to your suggestions and afterward hold resentment, making it much harder for you to serve them later on. Despite the fact that you might have the option to point out your anxiety delicately and carefully and mention your availability to serve them, sometimes the most beneficial and compassionate act is to permit them to confront the outcomes of their actions. There are additionally times when you simply need to wait until the one you care for exhibits readiness to change by approaching you or another person over the issue.

Finally, it is interesting to note one aftereffect of practicing this key: it makes the way for compassion for the despondent. We realize that nonvirtuous demonstrations depend on misdirected endeavors to find fulfillment.

In studying the locks and keys, we ought to make sure to apply them to ourselves.

We have to cultivate:

- Friendliness toward our own happiness. This is one instance in life when a little indulgence is acceptable, especially when our happiness has its underlying foundations in spiritual acts or qualities.
- Loving compassion for our own distress. Be kind to yourself.
- Joy when we manifest virtues.
- Strength, patience, and equanimity when working to eliminate our weaknesses. Forgiveness assumes an important job with this.

Sri Patanjali knows human instinct. There will consistently be somebody who will find an explanation not to take his suggestions. "It doesn't make a difference," he consoles us. "For whatever length of time that you find it spiritually inspiring, proceed. It will work."

The teachings of Raja YOGA are valuable for everybody, paying little heed to foundation, period, or faith tradition. If the picked object catches our interest, inspires and points us in the direction of the Self, it has Sri Patanjali's seal of endorsement.

Chapter 12: The benefits of YOGA sutras

A quick reminder of how true we need to practice and how it has helps us to gain back our strength and ease the stress of having an improved health. In the widest sense, Patanjali has helped us to see how to layout the real definition of YOGA.

How YOGA helps to comprehend to happiness. According to Patanjali's teaching, it helps us to see how our emotions get in the way with our happiness.

YOGA also helps to construct a lifelong practice, from the sets of information we have had from the research of YOGA and physical asana practice, though, YOGA sutras has decided to give us a wider view, to help us have a review of how big YOGA practice is. We look beyond its ability to help because as we grow, and a physical practice may not be performed. We acquire an extending and required relationship with YOGA that changes everything about our lives.

How living with YOGA can help us transform who we are as a person. Looking into how we live within the context of life as a whole. We don't just practice YOGA, but also a state of being. Patanjali gave us a piece of instruction on how to live a yogic life and the self conduct, so we can know and experience why we need to live in peace, integrity, and harmony without costing us anything even when we face difficulties.

Why we should connect to the lineage of YOGA. We as a learner receive teachings from a teacher, right? And how we should honor the fact that we are being taught, training is never easy but you have to put your best at it. With the study of sutras, we get to know better, to practice and teach more people about the history and tradition of YOGA.

When it comes to exaggerating the benefits of YOGA, it not just about a specific hundred of pictures and stories. A good idea is when you practice YOGA, not just about physical fitness and flexibility but how much YOGA had profound benefits.

Basically, YOGA has a lovely postures and physical benefits that you can see in someone who has done YOGA practice regularly.

How YOGA maintains a strong backbone, this backbone supports the [CNS] central nervous system that controls the cells of the body; it is the backbone that saves the spinal cord. It controls the function of the body and the mind. It helps to maintain a good posture.

Many YOGA asana of some that are specific for the spine, which is the backbone, that brings out nurturing awareness around the backbone to widen more.

Asana for a stronger backbone- savasana, supra pavanamuktasana, tadasana, Ardha uttarasana and so on. A YOGA practice can also improve functional skills in patients with less pain.

YOGA helps to improve because your body needs sleep just as it needs air and food to function at its best. During sleep, your body heals itself and restore its chemical balance. Insufficient can cause fatigue and depression-related problems. Few people about [sleeping disorder] insomnia because they don't consult their physician. YOGA is good for reducing arousal that causes insomnia when you make use of the relaxation postures and practice of meditation.

In weeks research on chronic insomnia patients, the patients would be asked to practice a YOGA meditation session by their own, at the end of this research, there is a significant improvement in sleep deficiency, the total sleep time, the total sleep time and the sleep onset latency, this is seen as a sleep-wake diary.

Many people think about YOGA as an activity that promotes balance and flexibility but also includes relaxation and breathing exercises and meditation.

YOGA helps in weight loss and irregular diet. Practice YOGA as often as possible as you can in order to lose weight, you can be more active on YOGA practice. Try to balance out your practice with a more relaxing and quiet class.

Don't weigh yourself directly after a YOGA class when you have had a hot YOGA class, since you may lose water weight during the class. Rather, weigh yourself at the same time. YOGA breathing techniques can also to burn belly fat.

YOGA also helps to enhance hair growth, hair loss can be our concern as human that involves a young age group that causes sensitive pain. Because of pregnancy, stress induces hormonal changes. We all have a dream of having a black and long hair, Thus, reducing hair damage and regrowth needs to be focused upon. To benefit the hair growth, you should try to mix YOGA with other anxiety decreasing techniques including the scalp massage. An increase in blood flow to the scalp contributes to hair growth.

YOGA prevents growing old too early

Growing old ie ageing is a system whereby the part of the body which is aging changes that is characterized by constant change. Wrinkled skin, grey hair, risk of diseases, these are likely common when it comes to ageing. When you're suggesting a natural anti-ageing therapy that would get you saved from side effects of chemical products that are being used for to delay ageing, YOGA is the one I would gladly recommend because YOGA has shown an analysis of achievement and outcomes in terms of improving the blood circulation, maintaining the youthful faces with a glowing skin that would also prevent premature ageing.

The increase of bone density is how we allow YOGA to do the work and strengthen the body.

YOGA brings flexibility to the muscles

Our body gets lazy when we have a slow-motion on how things are done or how we relate to the body itself by being sluggish that lessens the supple and increase of prone to injury. Muscles become atrophic and rigid.

The YOGA posture helps to decrease the tension from the body and mind. In a YOGA posture, during practice, you stretch the muscles and hold it in a YOGA posture, this would help to strengthen the muscles fibers.

YOGA practice also makes the nervous system activity,

a change in body posture confidence and better perception of the body.

Improvements in sexual function

YOGA postures enhance the core because it assists to have more power to control the pelvis that helps to also enhances the erection, increases the level of testosterone and enhances the libido (sex desires).

What do YOGA breathing techniques work for? It works for glowing the skin or preferably it glows the skin

YOGA breathing is also known as pranayama, which cleanses the blood and increases the supply of oxygen.

Here are the breathing techniques of YOGA; Bhasmari, Anulom Vilom, Kapalbhati and so on. Emphasizing the effect of asanas and resolve the skin by griefs of having tissue effects for detoxification.

Rising of oxygen information

Breathing is important and one of the most physiological method that pertains to air in and out of the lungs.

Breathing is possible through Prana, and if there's improper breathing, oxygen becomes small in the lungs.

With a consistent practice of yogic breathing (Pranayama), the intake of the oxygen can rise and its consumption can be lessening. There'San increase flow of the oxygen and different YOGA postures of bending enhances the pulmonary function.

YOGA enhances metabolism

Metabolism is a normal function of the body that includes a chemical reaction that helps in maintaining life.

Most people don't know that slow metabolism produces to burn fewer calories and they eat small foods to avoid weight gain. In most cases, we find it wrong to be thin or fat. So why you need is to burn fats and strengthen metabolism directly.

A Good Heart Functioning

The heart beats about 115,000 times each day and it comes around 50-100 beats per minute. What a figure, to know how always the heart functions.

When there's a stress in the heart, it causes a heart outbreak, B.P, and diabetes.

YOGA brings changes of better health to the system of the heart.

YOGA practice assists when it comes to pregnancy and the menstrual cycle.

Physical activity is done during pregnancy and the menstrual cycle in the form of YOGA suggested a sense of assurance and competence in a woman. When a woman involves herself in parental YOGA, there is a positive result of her having a better outcome on living conditions and parental care.

YOGA helps to reduce the blood pressure (H.B.P) and hypertension

Hypertension occurs when the blood in the arteries put in more powerful efforts with much pressure more than the standard value 130/80/hg

The H.B.P is a quiet killer when it shows off in the early stage and it comes to be very hard to observe its symptoms. Likewise, it affects the benefit of the heart and circulatory system by reducing the oxygen content in the blood.

How YOGA helps to increase pain tolerance

Pain can be emotional or physical depending on the case of injuries. YOGA attempts to the pain by carrying out neuroanatomical changes in the brain and increase the intra-insular connectivity.

Hence, YOGA increases the pain and change pain perception.

Lowering the blood sugar level by YOGA

Hormones made by the pancreas that allows the body to use sugar and keeps the blood sugar from getting too high or too low is Insulin.

YOGA has an encouraging on endocrine glands to ease the stress and distress that operates in the mechanism.

YOGA is mostly the practice of the mind that controls the emotional and mental benefits of YOGA

YOGA as a stress buster

Stress is obvious to itself in many aspects like mental, sensitive and physical. YOGA is useful when it comes to dealing with stress for relief for the reason that it lowers the stress hormone production and improves the production of endorphins.

YOGA brings positivity in life which can make you go through the strongest of moments. The right emotions can make you feel healthy, good and a smile on your face, with fewer chances of falling ill. YOGA is a practice that appeals to psychological well-being not just an exercise to build strength, lessen obese weight and so on. YOGA would have helped you by now with the help of reducing negative emotions and improvement positive emotions.

YOGA reduces opposing emotions and improve happiness in one's life.

Putting YOGA practice on a consistent basis increases the happiness hormones in the body, as I have stated earlier. YOGA practice has been verified by accomplishing goals and reducing stress and thus increases all-around happiness.

YOGA also boosts confidence, confidence that relies on how good you can or cannot do something, understanding your body about being confident is another aspect to know how well you are eligible to do something (in your soul, body, and mind)

With what you've been reading and learned so far, you can clarify that YOGA is known to teach its learners on how to totally and completely tune with their body.

YOGA had improved confidence by improving the physical and mental state of the body.

How YOGA increases Gray matter. The gray matter is one area of the brain that is associated with muscle control and plays a vital role in seeing, hearing, making decisions and so on. Also, it is associated with sensory perception. The more you practice YOGA, the higher the gray matter volume and the lower you practice YOGA, the lower is the gray matter volume.

YOGA also makes you focus

The efforts you pass through to achieve a particular thing, maybe your goal depends on your success which is measured by the efforts.

YOGA improves the focus and attention for those who practice consistently and also teaches learners how to focus their energies on the right part to ensure that their minds are more determined.

YOGA is a memory booster.

A memory of what you have learned is vital. We all don't have the same memory power, nevertheless, one of YOGA's practice is to boost memory.

How quick we react on time

Reaction time is mostly about how fast the mind

functions and takes quick action. Consider how it comes to be a necessary action to be quick and mentally thoughtful.

After a stretch with YOGA, the (Auditory Reaction Time) ART, (Visual Reaction Time) VRT, (Cutaneous Reaction Time) CRT, have a decrease in the alert. This simply implies that the bran will respond quickly to any clue from the body. Practically, YOGA has an encouraging effect on improving the body's reaction time.

Spiritual Benefits of YOGA

We grow spiritually, yes, because it allows us to explore the immensity of chances surrounding us.

Some good social skills

YOGA classes are fascinating whereby people with opinions, meet and practice together. Well, I suggest that these classes should be for introverts, people who are concerned with their own feelings and opinion.

YOGA teaches self-control intentionally which may be in an aspect of concentrating on a particular thing, letting go of anger.

YOGA teaches one how the Kundalini is awake

We can actually understand the hugeness of energy in a human body through the idea of kundalini.

Religiously, a yogi seeks to create awareness inside the body. Once kundalini is awake it is penetrated through different chakras that are currently along the backbone and finally got the top of the head.

How YOGA benefits when it comes to preventing a disease

Basically, YOGA has worked as a raw remedy to cure chronic disease and helps people to come out healthy and fine from a serious conditions. Practically, what can be done is a regular practice while YOGA cure the disease.

YOGA reduces the risk of Alzheimer's

A fearing illness during an old age is called dementia that's thinking and memory problem. It doesn't not just start at once, it happens to be a gradual process, slowly from the start and later it get worsen.

Minimizes the chances of diabetes

A lot of people have diabetes and most of these people are pre-diabetic, they are being set on a notice of having a higher risk of coming to be a diabetic patient sometimes in the future. With the hope of a lot of people, YOGA claims to assist them in knocking down the blood glucose levels.

YOGA also reduces heart disease

Pressure, worries and bad thoughts have increased the probability of heart disease. Chubbiness and diabetes can make the situation of having a heart disease worse.

With the help of YOGA practice, there's a chances of overcoming these disease with faith.

YOGA helps to reduce pain relief.

YOGA postures helps the body to be more flexible, loosen the joints that are tights. This same YOGA practice helps to keep the pain manageable.

No matter how addicted you are, with the help of YOGA, you are capable of quitting smoking, smoking is bad to the health and causes various injuries to our health, we all know how it has damage a lot of the kidney and the blood running through our body and yet a lot of people find it difficult to quit. YOGA can be analyzed to adjust treatment for terminating smoking.

YOGA reduces difficulties and distraction to the body by directing your energy to other useful areas.

In conclusion

YOGA is not a difficult discipline to follow, attend and pursue, just go with the flow and attend your practice consistently.

The results would come out well and fine.

Chapter 13: The best practices in YOGA Sutras

You might be so bored; how can I be of help? Do you suggest that we should go on a YOGA practice? A YOGA practice can be easy to fix with the help of YOGA sutras. Let's explore how the YOGA practice can be done on your own even without guidance or instructions. Here are the five YOGA sutras to help you enhance your YOGA practice; YOGA is the control [nirodhah, coordination, quieting] of the adaption [the thoughts pattern] of the mind.

The eight limbs; is the code of self- regulation [yamas], practices of self training [niyamas,] postures [asana], prana [pranayama], withdrawal of the sense [pratyahara], concentration [dharana], meditation [dhyana], and perfected concentration [Samadhi].

The inner concentration which is stated on the process of receptiveness experience that is done in a way that leads towards higher sense perception. It is also leads to the stability of the mind.

The five varieties of the thought pattern to observe are 1] to know the right thing correctly [pramana] 2]to recollect the memory [smriti] 3] deep sleep [nidra] 4] not knowing the correct thing [viparyaya] 5] imagination [vikalpa].

YOGA in form of action [kriya YOGA]in from of three parts; the selfstudy in the teaching [svadhyaya], the devotion [ishvara pranidhana] and the training and cleansing of the sense.

What I would suggest is that, set a timer while your phone is on a no call mood, roll ou your mat and lie on it, bend your knees, spread your feet to the edge of the mat, in this case, you shouldn't use a big mat, then gently move your knees together , close your eyes and your hand should be on your belly. You can now think about the idea of atha, listen and be silent.

Sutra 2.31 translation; it is a simple concept to be kind to people but most people find it difficult to practice, try as much as possible to put your best to it and act from a place of compassion.

Sutras 2.32 translation; purity and cleanliness of the body and mind, an attitude of discipline and studying on sacred words. To practice self training. Take care of yourself physically and mentally, loving yourself and caring for yourself is important and also part of the YOGA practice, including healthy life. They guide you through your perception.

Sutras 2.46 translation; perfecting your posture, relaxing, making your attention to merge with endlessness. This is the practice most people visualize when they think of YOGA. Ie the physical posture you do on the math, it is not about seeing what the person next to you is doing but it is about what your body can do at the moment while using the physical practice as an attitude of calmness and relief.

Sutras 2.49 translation; once you have gotten your posture right, you will start including breath control or pranayama. The physical practice is incomplete without the breath and can be disconnected from the focus and control.

Sutras 2.54 translation; when your sense and action quit to be involved with the connected objects in your mental domain and find its way to into the consciousness from where it occurred, it is called pratyahara , which is the fifth step.

Your perception of the world is unique.

Sutras 3.1 translation; the process of fixing together of your mind attention is concentration. You can teach yourself to be discipline by silencing your mind which increase the focus and reduce the stress.

With your understanding of meditation, you should see meditation as an aspect that is thought of as separate, and also a valuable tool that helps you grow your understanding of YOGA.

Sutra 3.3 translation; when the importance of an object or point of focus stick to your mind, the intense concentration is called Samadhi. Deep concentration would require practice and focus but they end up leading to another way of thinking, vision about yourself and your standing point to the world.

Sutra 3.49 translation; with your ability over the sense, your thoughts and action comes the haste of the mind. Having control over the mind and the body.

Getting familiar with sutras itself is a good way of getting closer to your YOGA practice.

Atha YOGA anushasam; atha which means to draw close your attention, allow atha to be your mantra while you practice now. Use this ability to draw close your attention and awareness to the true teaching of YOGA.

YOGA citta vritti nirodhah; being conscious and ability to calm your mind, as human beings, feelings, thoughts and emotions flow and travel through our minds, this verse encourages you to become the diviner of your mind through the practice of YOGA. Meditate on this verse by observing the contents of your mind.

Abhyasa vairagyabhyam tan nirodhah; patanjalis focus is to calm the mind completely, holding strong and letting go that seems like two opposing action, it brings ease when following the practice of YOGA. You begin to notice moments and actions where your mind attaches to one thing.

Tatra athitau yatnah abhyasa; patanjali explains that the only way to teach calmness of mind is to practice with effort.

Isvara pranidhana; patanjali make a references the state of samadhire where things come together, in your practice today make yourself to turn everything to deeper believe.

Taj japas tad artha bhavanam; patanjali believes that the divine rest is in the Om, reciting Om would help you become more closer to the true nature of yourself.

Atah pratyakcetanadhigamah api antarayabhavas ca; [YOGA sutras; chapter 1 vs 29] when the inner consciousness is revealed, our obstacles reduce and we come to realize and know the true self. As you meditate on this verse, you would begin to notice the lessening of the difficulties.

It is important to understand the functions of the mind to identify the functioning one at the moment. These sutras explain how YOGA is a way of working the mind and through the practice you can find your true self like I mentioned earlier. With efforts and discipline, you can be on the right part of YOGA with a fully awakened mind.

Basically, the purpose of YOGA practice is to bring out the calmness and coolness of the mind, now that you've known what and how to practice the YOGA I am sure it would make you stay healthy to your satisfaction and the health would help free some space to work in your mind. You don't practice YOGA for the fun of it and you don't practice to benefit health only. The end goal must be a freedom from the turn and switch of mind to be a YOGA practice.

The word YOGA is applied to physical activities that are more of a training or exercise. Which of these are you doing? The question is for you to ask yourself.

Most people come to YOGA because of the physical benefits because the physical practice is fun, and that's what most people like, I must say. Even though that is not the problem, but the problem is when we multiply the myth or misconception of the practice which is usually done by YOGA teachers all because they want to empower the name "YOGA" and its vogue.

Samadhi pada defines YOGA and puts the practice in opinion.

Sadhana pada: provides the essential framework and covers the yamas, niyamas, asana, and pranayama.

The Pranayama is the gateway to the inner world.

Vibhuti pada: takes over where sadhana pada leaves off. Beginning with pratyahara, it deals with the way to proceed our awareness, dharana, dhyana and samadhi.

Kaivalya pada; in the final pada, patanjali brings together many of more magical powers and most times difficult to understand teachings of the practice.

At the beginning of the YOGA sutras, Patanjali lays out the context of practice, immediately after lecturing the need for practice, the process, and the goals, he expresses the features of his entire message in the first three sutras.

Sutras 1:1atha YOGAnushāsanam begins the instruction on the YOGA practice

Atha explains the encouraging nature of teachings. Translated as "Now", atha is also the expression of the guiding opinion that that lives in the heart and the mind of human being. The meaning of " Now" is in itself auspicious. Now is the existing moment and place of no future and no past.

Sutras 1:2

YOGAsh chitta nirodhah YOGA is the ability of roaming tendencies of the mind.

In this sutras, Patanjali states the issues: vrittis - habitual activities of individual consciousness that increase and decrease in the mind.

Vrittus have the power to keep us locked into the littleness of self consciousness to the larger frame work.

Suras 1:3

Tada drashtuh svarupe vasthanam and the divine becomes traditional in it's vital nature.

The third sutras explain what happens when we calm the vrittis in the mind.

"Seer" is the term Patanjali uses to donate Unmanifest awareness.

Patanjali explain to us that the seer is the only true eyewitness. When vrittis are allowed to run widespread, the brightness of awareness hardly shines through the difficulty and waste of mind.

The area of which individual consciousness is cloudy with thoughts and feelings, and that person is thoroughly distracted from seeing the deep aspect of truth. But when the vrittis are illustrated, they no longer cloud someone's consciousness.

Chapter 14: Best times of the day to do YOGA

Do you wonder why the time of the day matters? It is a nice idea of having the best times of the day to do your YOGA practice. The purpose of YOGA is to develop you.

The Ideal YOGA Time: to be honest, practicing YOGA at the shift between day and night is better because during these times, the day is shifting and the energy is shifting with it.

In this case, your location matters because of the temperature which can be more moderate and there is less heat in the environment. You can align your body and energy with the changes happening in your environment at the transition points in the day.

Timing: Experienced yogis can put you into more detail. For spiritual progress, the time of the day is before sunrise, at the Brahma Muhurta, the last section in the night. This can be between 3 am until sunrise.

I'm sure you would be interested in progressing your physical YOGA practice, then the Sandhya Kalas (shifting in the day to night) is really the acceptable time to practice.

Practicing YOGA at any time of the day depending on your choice and environment is better than not practicing at all, YOGA is never a bad idea to practice any time of the day. People are different as well as their body too, so if you're not a morning person, don't be discouraged by not practicing YOGA when you can.

YOGA practice is recommended in the morning or early evening. Why? Because a morning YOGA can be completely active and consist of an extensive practice. So, always finish with Savasana (Corpse Pose) no matter the time of the day you practice.

Practically, the best time to do YOGA is the time that works best for you. You need to find a routine that fits your lifestyle and also work alongside with your schedule. It changes over time as your life changes.

For instance, I attend a YOGA class at my best time according to the draft time, most especially after work, I attended this class for years but when I started having kids, it makes more sense to me going during the day while they are in school. I practice YOGA at different times and different days, all because I find a routine that is sustainable for me.

Try as much as possible to fix in YOGA into your schedule.

Some YOGA traditions such as the Ashtanga system of Pattabhi Jois, doing YOGA asanas early in the morning before the sunrise. Most of Ashtanga home practitioners stick to this routine.

Practicing YOGA in the morning makes one work better at one's vocation. While in the evening it removes the exhaustion of the day's stress and makes one fresh and calm.

Both times sound good, right? But whatever time of the day it may be, it is very important that the bowels must be emptied before attempting asana.

While an early morning practice has so many things to submit with, including the compatibility of doing YOGA with an empty stomach and bowels with the virtue of getting the day off with a good onset. The fact that you don't want to get up before the break of daylight doesn't mean you should write off YOGA. You may be tougher but have stability in the morning, while you're more limber but tired in the twilight.

Make a schedule of the right time of the day is important if you try to establish a home practice. Either morning or evening can be a practice time for working folks. The morning routine can help to lessen into your day so as to start on the right foot while an evening practice helps you wind down.

If you want your schedule to stick, you would also need to stick to your schedule.

You don't need to worry too much about someone less idea of the best time for YOGA, just find time that works best for you before looking out for others.

The traditional view of practicing YOGA is in the morning, before the sun rises and before breakfast. One of the advantages to it is that, it can be a perfect way to start your day with mindful awareness for the rest of the day. Connecting yourself first can place you in a position of mental strength that has potential throughout the whole day but physically, it can awake your body and release tension of the sleep.

You don't do mornings? You don't have to bother. There are times that morning practice is not desirable or even possible. But some people's body grievance physical movement which is true for anyone that suffers with back pain. YOGA may help, if you're willing to do it, or is uncertain to be a pleasant experience which may even put you off to practice YOGA altogether.

Practically, there are more reasons why morning practice may not work, maybe someone who has families, early morning office work, this may not carve out their practice time.

I would suggest that you should set your alarm to an hour earlier and if it's unhelpful it is also not practical for you to go to bed an hour earlier.

A great idea is making a mindful start for the day. Before getting out of bed, a five minutes seats mediation and mindful breathing is better than nothing done.

One of the things I love doing is meditating first while my mind is at its quickest, after some hours on my phone or PC, YOGA is an exact thing to stretch out the body and bring it back to itself.

Late afternoon before dinner can actually be chosen by you and it's the best and lovely time to do YOGA. It's almost like a ceremony to give a remark at the end of your working day and your transition into more relaxed time and can boost up your appetite for the evening meal. But most people believe that YOGA at the end of the day feels better for their body, the best thing you can do to yourself is to fix in your schedule for YOGA.

Finally, the late evening, just before going to bed. It can be an optimum time for your YOGA practice. Let's find something that suits your life.

Conclusion

Now, we have gotten to the end of this book. One more question to answer, 'Why Raja YOGAs?' Raja simply means a king, a king that is capable of acting independently with dignity and assurance. Well, Raja YOGA is organized in different parts and also referred to as a "classical YOGA" which is the ancient system developed into a joint practice. During the second century the Raja YOGA was compiled by the sage patanjali in his famous YOGA Sutras.

Different people see things differently and refer to things according to their own understanding simply that, some see YOGA as a spiritual practice while some see it as a faithful religious practice.

YOGA is organized in different parts.

Yama - Self Control which consist of five principle.

Satya which means the truthfulness: Conveying the truth matters and speaking the truth is awesome. Basically, we can cloth a truth with loving words and also the other way round which is yelling the truth at someone, all because you don't want to hide your feelings, not to make excuses about being truthful.

Our conscious is a witness who knows our inner truth.

Ahisma - Non-Violence

Not to cause harm and pain to any living being by thought or word.

Nonviolence which means not to kill. The death of an

animal is the consumption of meat, animals has instincts most especially when they sense that they are to be killed, they would be in mortal fear and stress hormones which are released throughout their body. These hormones stay in the flesh of the animal being killed and eaten by unsuspecting people.

Asteya which means not to steal things that belong to the rightful owner, not materials things only but also stealing someone's opportunity, hope, happiness, robbing someone's property.

Brahmacharya - Pure way

Brahmacharya which means our thought should be one towards God but doesn't implies that we should neglect our rights and duties to the world. But also fulfilling the responsibilities with care and with awareness which means God is the doer.

Aparigrapha – Nonassociation with Possessions

One has many possessions alongside with many worries. Leaving this world with nothing all because we came with nothing, so we leave all. It also means to grant other people freedom and not to hold onto others by freeing ourselves.

Niyama which consist of five principles;

Shauca – purity, not just the external purity but also the inner purity, you should get to see that our mind, body, feelings and thoughts should also be pure as well. We should also keep people with great influence around us, people who are spiritual and willing to support with their wisdom, this means, man is a product of influence.

Svadhyaya means our study to the holy scriptures; all well and good as YOGA aspirant we ought to keep ourselves detailed with the scriptures of the YOGA philosophy that include the Bhagavad gita, the YOGA sutras of patanjali and so on. They provide assistant and knowledge to our YOGA part.

Tapa which means self discipline; life has its own ups and downs, the good and the bad, so when we encounter obstacles, we should hold on firm and never give up. Instead of giving up we should rather continue on our chosen part that leads to success with a strong sense of purpose and determination. One of the keys to success is patience and perseverance.

Our pure devotion to god matters because god surrender with trust and faith to the honest one.

Santosh- contentment

Inner discontent destroys all wealth even if you possess all mines of gold. Contentment is the biggest wealth we are able to possess.

Raja YOGA achieve the control of mind with the physical

exercise which is asana, and the breath exercise which is the pranayama. It leads to the inner power that are awake and will continue to give guidance on the spiritual part.

The withdrawal of the sense which is known as the pratyahara; as human we can withdraw our sense from external objects and also regain our sense consciously with full awareness.

Keeping the body as we practice pratyahara in the first stage of meditation, by keeping our body motionless, our eyes closed and our mind quiet and we pay attention to directed inward. While observing the sound, with a gradual process our awareness is withdrawn to one inner space, the sound within the body like our heart beat, blood circulation and so on. Mastering these steps of pratyahara will help us to progress our concentration.

Dharana which means to focus on our thought and feeling upon single objects, usually we conquer this for a short time then our thoughts distract us. As humans, we lose concentration in few minutes until we are eligible to concentrate on a thought or feeling for a long time.

Dhyana which means meditation, we don't learn meditation as we cannot learn how to sleep, the sleeps comes when we are relaxed and our body is quiet, so meditation happens when our mind is quiet. So more reasons why we need to feed on the positive because our brains reproduce only on what we feed into it but in meditation all we experience is pure being, the moments the intellect is peaceful and all the ego ceases to exist , a divine light shines within our heart and we are one with it. A brain cannot be compared with a computer that has enormous storage capacity.

A yogi arrives at the end and become one with supreme consciousness and the yogi consciousness that founds peace, bliss and quiet eternal.

This experience cannot be described in words because; someone who has loved knows what love is and someone who is in pain knows what the pain is, their feelings are different and so only one who has experienced Samadhi knows what Samadhi is.

The union of the individual soul with the cosmic soul is the goal of YOGA.

As I continue with what YOGA entails, raja YOGA can be viewed as a royal part in other to attain the state of unity with the mind, body and spirit. while hatha YOGA was developed as a preparation for raja YOGA, they can be practiced simultaneously.

The dos and don'ts of raja YOGA was stated earlier, yama, the respects of others which includes non-violence trust and so on. As patanjali instructed that one should find a comfortable yet stable seated position with a slow deep breath which is obtained, then you have started practicing the internal limbs which is; dharana, dhyana, pratyahara and Samadhi. Pratyahara work is to draw the mind focus away from outer senses to the inner sensations of the body, once this is achieved, then the next limb, dharana which is used to concentrate the mind on one single objects, usually the breath. This pratice becomes more challenging, keeping the mind focus and releasing the attachments to thought. Once you obtain the ability to concentrate on a single object to a point whereby you are absorbed in it, the you can move to the next limb of dhyana meditation.

Still on who YOGA is, YOGA has suffered from spiritual poverty of the modern world which has been trivialized. The essence of YOGA has been misrepresented and has been put together for profits by smart people who actually think they are wise though. In another context, YOGA has been presented as a cult religion with the aim of attracting followers.

YOGA defines itself as a science which is practical and has systematic discipline and has a goal of helping people with the aim of making them know their true nature which is not part of a religious process.

Religious seek explain what we should believe while a practical science such as meditation is based on experienced of what teachers had gone through and yogis who have used techniques to experience their deepest self. YOGA itself does not intrude any religion and may be practiced by anyone who wants to. YOGA has been practiced in the east and west, basically it can be seen as an error to consider YOGA as an Eastern import. YOGA is relevant to the modern world for creating a sense of inner peace, clarity and harmony of mind. To cut the long story short, YOGA has been a tool for survival to expand the joy in our lives.

The Living Traditional; though, YOGA doesn't belong to

the east according to research, but it is easy to trace the root of YOGA there because the cultural change did not hide the origins of the science. No one invented YOGA, but YOGA is a living traditional that is practiced back for centuries. What we have learnt so far and what we are still learning about YOGA is that, it has to do with our nature as human. The very word YOGA makes reference to, the root yuj [unity or yoke] which simply means the purpose of YOGA is to unite ourselves as one with our highest nature. We also see that amid our success in the external world we have achieved little of lasting value. These problems cannot be solved through new technological developments.

The various path of YOGA includes; hatha YOGA that deals with the body and breathing exercise which helps the student to become more aware of his or her inter sense and also hatha YOGA exercise build a strong and healthy body.

Karma YOGA, it teaches us to do our duties in life skillfully and selflessly with the dedication of our result in action to humanity. So, when we practice this aspect of YOGA it helps us and leads us to live successfully without being a burden.

Jnana YOGA leads to a path of knowledge and wisdom. This is mainly for a few fortune people who are aware of the higher realities of life.

Mantra YOGA it involves the meditation and the use of certain sounds called mantras which is discovered in an intense meditation by highly advance teachers. Mantras helps students for self-purification and concentration.

Kundalini YOGA, a technical science and a guidance of competent teacher that helps to awaken the vital force that remains dormant in the body.

We have refined our desires, emotions and thoughts by following this part methodically.

The Royal Part; raja YOGA teaches from different parts and can be practiced by people of many background. It involves three importance of human interactions; the physical, mental and spiritual, by following these parts, we aim to achieve harmony and realization of one self.

Raja YOGA can also be called ashtanga which is mainly the process of self transformation on the same level of physical body with the most subtle of life. The eight steps of YOGA are the, niyama, dharana, niyama, pratyahara, asana, dhayana, Samadhi and pranayama which are explained above.

Raja YOGA is an ancient system of religious understanding and study that helps us to get back to our state of inner peace and self –worth by lighting the soul's virtues.

Our clearer sense of purpose and inner stability and a few moment of silence each day remind of us who we are, it reminds us of our purpose in life and our aim is to live together with honour, respects, trust, dignity and tolerance. The self respect which is a state of the inner dignity that brings benefit to one self.

No matter what life offers you, no matter the ups and down, you have to look after your self respect carefully to ensure yourself that you never lose it.

Raja YOGA. With the help of raja YOGA, we can use soul power to cure our ailments at the brahma kumaris centers which is close to your home. From experience, I have been practicing raja YOGA for the past 13 years which has helped me to stay safe from ailments like stomach pain, weakness, headache and temperature and so on, but most importantly is the joy and happiness we achieve from it while we study raja YOGA. Physical exercise should be done to remain healthy but we mostly forget to the mental exercise that is more beneficial as compared to the physical exercise.

With my experience of writing this book, we all have learnt from practical life experience, books and tv but at the same time we should not forget that God has made his way to the earth to teach us raja YOGA that helps us to clean our soul and mind with a clean and pure heart. As human beings we depend on doctors and medicine, most of us are not ready to listen to what God has in stock for us to kill our ailments, simply because we don't have faith. We are not conscious when we become careless about small ailments that results to big ailments such as cancer, kidney problem and so on. More reasons why we need God to help us cure our ailment and make us clean and free from ailments with the intake of raja YOGA meditation process and we become physically and mentally strong.

We need to understand very well because there is a seven days course that would be given to every soul that visits the Brahma kumaris centre and after seven days any soul that feels good will come regularly and join the Brahman Kumaris family, people who don't feel good and comfortable about the peace and joy of it would go away. The knowledge of Raja YOGA is understood by people who have more number of births and rebirths. The more the rebirths, the easier it becomes to understand raja YOGA and the more we practice the raja YOGA, the more we listen to the murli at the brahma kumaris centre. The process of curing any ailment through raja YOGA is slow but it is very effective, when we focus on the study of raja YOGA, the ailments would get removed and we become strong and healthy. Good things take time, so the fact that the process is slow does not mean we should lose faith and nit focus, all we have to do to get a better result is to pray and have faith, you should not expect a magic from the raja YOGA treatment. The raja YOGA meditation is a form that is convenient to people of all backgrounds. A meditation that doesn't involve rituals and can be practice at any time. The raja YOGA meditation is practiced with open eyes that makes the method easy and simple to practice. Religious awareness helps to give the power to determine the good and positive thoughts over the negative and wasteful ones. Rather than reacting to them, we respond to situations and we begin to live in peace to create a happy and healthy living that changes our lives to the positive way.

The more we spread the knowledge, the stronger we become.

Every one of these sutras begin with the word "or." They are the "oars" that assist us with rowing to the shore of harmony.

Or that quiet is retained by the controlled exhalation or retention of the breath.

The mind and breath are connected. At the point when the mind is quiet, so is the breath. At the point when the breath gets agitated, the mind follows. At the point when we direct the breath, the mind will turn out to be more clear and quiet. By delicately extending the duration of exhalations and continuously increasing the retention of the breath, we apply an incredible calming influence on the mind.

(A note of caution: breath retention is an extremely incredible practice. To avoid any potential physical damage, it ought to be endeavored uniquely under the guidance of a qualified educator.) Or that (undisturbed calmness) is attained when the perception of an unobtrusive sense object arises and holds the mind consistent.

For certain seekers, the experience of something strange goes about as a support to drive forward in their practices. Tradition recommends a few different ways to gain the experience of unpretentious sense perceptions: consistent spotlight on the tip of the nose or tongue, for example. If your concentration is sufficiently profound and stable, you will experience a nice scent with the first technique and a great taste with the second.

Or by concentrating on the supreme, ever-blissful Light within.

This sutra alludes to meditation using a visualization technique. From this we can infer that any inspiring visualization, religious image, or form of God that points to the Self can be a piece of a YOGA practice.

We are approached to concentrate our minds on a

reality that we have not yet experienced (that there is a Divine Light within). It requires a certain amount of faith even to attempt this. In the long run, the visualized Light will disappear and be supplanted with the genuine experience.

Or by concentrating on an extraordinary soul's mind which is completely liberated from connection to detect objects.

This can be viewed as an alternative to the above sutra. If you can't imagine or believe in your own Inner Light, at that point look to the core of an incredible saint, prophet, or yogi in whom you have faith. Maybe you can perceive the Light there.

Or by concentrating on an insight had during dream or profound rest.

This sutra is referring to a particular sort of dream: those that are spiritually uplifting, that here and there influence us for the better or show us a supportive exercise.

With respect to profound rest, Sri Patanjali is not asking us to meditate on rest itself however on the tranquility of dreamless rest.

Or by meditating on anything one picks that is elevating.

Sri Patanjali knows human instinct. There will consistently be somebody who will find an explanation not to take his suggestions. "It doesn't make a difference," he consoles us. "For whatever length of time that you find it spiritually inspiring, proceed. It will work."

The teachings of Raja YOGA are valuable for everybody, paying little mind to foundation, time, or faith tradition. If the picked object catches our interest, inspires and points us in the direction of the Self, it has Sri Patanjali's seal of endorsement.

Step by step, one's dominance in concentration stretches out from the littlest particle to the best magnitude.

Through faithful practice, the yogi can concentrate the mind on any part of creation, from the most unobtrusive to the unthinkably immense. A mind with this level of center and clarity is fit for meditating on the Infinite.

The following sutra begins a series of four on the topic of samadhi.

Similarly, as the normally pure precious stone accept shapes and colors of articles set close to it, so the yogi's mind, with its absolutely corrected modifications, turns out to be clear and adjusted and attains the state devoid of differentiation between knower, comprehensible, and information. This culmination of meditation is samadhi.

For what reason would we wish to experience a "state devoid of differentiation between knower, comprehensible, and information?"

Perception requires three factors: the knower; an item to perceive; and the demonstration of knowing. This triple procedure is helpful for obtaining ordinary information however is insufficient for experiencing unpretentious parts of Prakriti and for attaining of Self-realization.

Samadhi is the zenith of the meditative procedure in which the "differentiation between knower, comprehensible, and information" dissolves. It is state in which insight is gained through union with the object of contemplation. The mind, consistent and clear as a crystal, temporarily gives up its self-identity and appears to vanish as it permits the object of meditation alone to shine forth.

In the following three sutras, Sri Patanjali extends the discussion of samadhi by examining two of the four samprajnata samadhis introduced in sutra 1.17: vitarka and vichara. Vitarka samadhi is divided into two categories: with (sa) and past (nir) examination. In the same way, vichara can be either with or past insight.

The samadhi in which an item, its name, and applied information on it are mixed is called savitarka samadhi, the samadhi with examination.

Savitarka samadhi is absorption on a gross item; one that can be perceived by the ordinary detects. This absorption initiates an unconstrained and intuitive examination of the qualities of the item mulled over. There is union with the object of contemplation, however it is mixed or interspersed with the word used to designate the item alongside our educated information on that object.

Savitarka samadhi likewise brings an intuitive understanding of the wonder of sense perception. What we experience as the simple perception of any item is a mixture of three distinct segments:

- Name (sabda): this is the "handle" that we use to get a handle on outside objects.
- Object (artha): this is the original object of perception as it exists.
- Knowledge (jnana): this is the reaction in the chitta to the object

We for the most part don't perceive an outer object directly. Knowledge obtained in the ordinary way is the consequence of the faculties relaying the vibrations of an object into the mind-stuff, which responds by forming vrittis. What we perceive is not the outside object but rather the risen modifications in the mind. In addition, past impressions identified with that object spring up. The aggregate of this reaction in the chitta is "con-ceptual" knowledge. Calculated knowledge can be a mix of precise and incorrect ideas regarding the object under examination. Generally, this triple procedure occurs so quickly that the means obscure into what is by all accounts the single occasion we call perception.

For example, there is the outer reality of a cow, the word "dairy animals" that we use to think about issues bovine, and ideas about cows—that they moo, give milk, and bite their cud. We are not normally mindful of the three distinct factors. We simply "see" a cow, and a wide range of related ideas show up in the mind.

In savitarka samadhi, the mind steadily figures out how to isolate and concentrate on the object itself, leaving behind the relativities of our knowledge of it and its name. This readies the mind for the following stage in samadhi: nirvitarka.

Examples of objects of meditation in this category are

the form of a deity, a light flame, or the rehashed sound of a mantra (instead of its unpretentious essential vibration).

At the point when the subconscious is very much purified of memories (regarding the object of contemplation), the mind seems to lose its own identity, and the object alone shines forth. This is nirvitarka samadhi, the samadhi past examination.

This is the second of the two tarka samadhis. The prefix, nir, signifies "without," yet with regards to the YOGA Sutras, it might be best comprehended as "past."

As with savitarka samadhi, the object of contemplation is an object perceptible by the faculties. Nirvitarka samadhi differs in that the object is currently completely known, so the procedure of "examination" is finished and henceforth stops.

In nirvitarka samadhi, the name of the object and any perceptual knowledge of it that was filtered (and therefore slanted or limited) through ordinary points of view stop to be influential factors in cognition. We are left with simply the object as it exists, uncol-ored by any past impressions we have of it. The subjective experience of nirvitarka samadhi is that the mind gives up its own identity for the purpose of union of the individual with the object of contemplation.

In the same way, savichara (with insight) and nirvichara (past insight) samadhis, which are practiced upon inconspicuous objects, are explained.

The two chara samadhis equal the tarka samadhis

aside from that the objects of contemplation are unpretentious components (tanmatras, for example, the energies or potentials that make sound, contact, taste, color, and sight possible, as opposed to objects perceivable by the faculties.

Specifically, savichara samadhi begins the procedure of comprehend ing the causes that brought the object into being: the inconspicuous components and the factors of reality.

Nirvichara samadhi is said to be "past insight," meaning that there are no further insights into the idea of the object to be had. There is finished knowledge of the object of contemplation down to its unobtrusive quintessence.

The nuance of possible objects of concentration closes just at the undifferentiated.

The mind gains the ability to center and converge with each object in creation, down to undifferentiated Prakriti.

All these samadhis are sabija [with seed].

The "seeds" are the subconscious impressions remaining in the mind. They can grow whenever, given the best possible time, spot, circumstance, and karma. At the point when they do grow, they can deprive the mind of the intuitive knowledge of samadhi and revive the door to the influence of ignorance and egoism.

In the pure clarity of nirvichara samadhi, the supreme Self shines.

In spite of the fact that not conferring liberation, nirvichara samadhi, by virtue of its purifying action on the subconscious mind, permits the Self to consider undistorted the mind. A unique and inconspicuous wisdom rises up out of nirvichara samadhi...

This is ritambhara prajna [the truth-bearing wisdom].

Ritambhara prajna: ritam, "truth," bhara, "bearing," and prajna, "wisdom, knowledge," consequently ritambhara prajna, the intuitive wisdom that is truth-bearing.

Sri Patanjali proceeds to grow our understanding of this special condition of knowing.

The motivation behind this special wisdom is different from the insights gained by investigation of consecrated tradition and inference.

Nirvichara samadhi opens the door to Self-realization. In this samadhi, the Self plainly considers the mind and gives a fact bearing wisdom: the discernment of Purusha from Prakriti. This discernment can't be achieved through investigation and inference. Its source is the intuitive insight of nirvichara samadhi.

Different impressions are overwhelmed by the impression created by this samadhi.

This samadhi creates ground-breaking subconscious impressions that incline the mind toward uninterrupted stillness, authority, and ultimately spiritual union. "Different impressions" mentioned in this sutra, the ones that are survived, are those that maintain the mind's profoundly ingrained habit of remotely oriented behavior. The explanation that nirvichara samadhi has this overpowering impact on lifetimes of inactive subconscious impressions is on the grounds that the impressions it produces are "truth-bearing," supercharged with the reality and immediacy of the Self.

As brilliant as this samadhi may be, there is still one more advance to climb. Nirvichara samadhi is a dualistic state. Indeed, even the feeling "I have realized the Absolute" should be abandoned. In spite of the fact that the image of the Absolute we see is thoroughly engrossing, it is a reflection, a duplicate, not the original. We have not yet realized that we are what we view. The final advance is the amazing quality of the mind and the realization of our True Identity as the Self. This realization is described in the following sutra.

With the stilling of even this impression, each impression is wiped out, and there is nirbija [seedless] samadhi.

The finite mind can't get a handle on the Infinite. The mind should be risen above to arrive at the final stage, nirbija samadhi. Indeed, even the impression left by nirvichara samadhi should be risen above. With both conscious mental activity and subconscious impressions (samskaras) totally stilled, the mind achieves (more correctly, realizes) ideal union with the Self. The universe and self liquefy into the experience of Oneness.

In the Vedas, this reality is communicated as: "Brahman [God or the Absolute] is One without a second." That implies, all that there is, is God. Normally, we can't think of a single unit of something without comparing it to at any rate one more. For example, it is impossible even to comprehend one apple (the oneness or singularity of it) except if we can contrast it with two or more apples. Indeed, even to comprehend the idea of nothing, we additionally need to contrast it with something. Similarly, we can't comprehend the oneness of the Absolute using the mind, which works just with dualities and relativities.

Nirbija samadhi is the experience of complete oneness with the Absolute. Hence, you will find out that you were neither alive nor dead, you neither did exist or not exist, you are the Absolute, you are the beginning and you are the end. You are the Self.